MW00634109

keep AN eye TO Ye
Sky !

Best,

Tom Warn

Praise for Tom Warner's

BEYOND THE STARS

"As a producer and director who has worked on multiple skeptical-type series, I have not always believed in the personal encounter stories of UFOs or para-normalities. That is, until working with Tom Warner. His story and version of the Berkshire UFO case is honest, raw, and haunting. It makes you question everything and is a must read."

—Joshua E. Kessler, *Unsolved Mysteries*

"Tom dives deep into the far-reaching effects that his extraordinary encounter set in motion. A tell-tale remarkable story well told by the author."

—Martin Willis, *Podcast UFO*

"I have had the privilege of working in the entertainment business for over 50 years. It was my honor to have worked with Tom Warner, an artist, a painter, and now the author of a phenomenal new book *Beyond The Stars*, a story about the boy, the abduction, the survival, and the man."

—Al Cooley, *Ghosts in The Valley*

"A vivid, extraordinary, firsthand account of the phenomena that engulfed the life of ten-year-old Tommy Warner. A must read."

—Nik Hunter, *UFO Chronicles Podcast*

"I have converted a nonbeliever after explaining your experience."

—Matt Elliot, Dark Sky Productions

"Tom Warner's bravery to speak about his experiences has helped others come forward. I hope this will start helping the world to learn the truth about what truly exists in the universe.

—Kellie Hunter, YouTube Channel *Third Eye - Question Everything*

"Tom Warner was woven into the tapestry of the unexplained and he has embraced it in a way few could."

—Bo Kennedy, *The Bump Podcast*

"Your program and your words brought me validation and peace."

—Cheryl Thompson, Fairview Hospital, Great Barrington, MA

BEYOND THE STARS

BEYOND THE STARS

TOM WARNER

Copyright © 2020 by Tom Warner.

All rights reserved. Published by WarnerArt.

Hardcover ISBN: 978-0-578-75527-4
eBook ISBN: 978-0-578-75528-1

Internal layout and copyediting by Courtney Larkin.

To my family: Christine, Katie, and Dan.
Thank you for being there on my bizarre journey!

Listen to the Angels, Fly with the Aliens
by Tom Warner

September arrived in '69
to shock and despair.
You don't want me, I begged.
Fear not child, fear not.
Why me, why me?
For the love of God, why me?
A forever repeating question,
time and time again,
those hidden lessons
among the leaves and rocks.
Sunrise to sunset I listened to my soul.
Stillness became me there in nature and life.
A telepathic voice, a gift given,
always to answer the call.
A bizarre journey filled with the unexplained.
Hear me, for I hear you
over the lapping waves on my shore.
Time and time again brought to the edge of life.
Death in the valley, I weep not for
lessons learned to pass on forever more.
May humanity listen and learn,
your voice always a reminder:
Listen to the angels, fly with the aliens.

-

Forward

How does one explain the unexplainable, and what purpose does it reveal, not only about the about subject of UFOs, but about the question I get most frequently asked: why Tommy Warner? I never intended to write my autobiography, but over time I felt compelled to express this complex story of an amazing event and life that followed afterwards.

After being asked to be on a number of radio shows and two documentaries, I began to think that perhaps I should examine the question of why I was chosen to experience all these bizarre happenings. My UFO encounters and my unusual journey did not start with that historic day of September 1, 1969, nor finish with that day. The commencement of this story started at such a young age and continued through my adulthood. I am but a messenger, and I will conclude the story with that message.

My book will take you from my youth and what I experienced before my close encounters, then to the encounters themselves and how I felt, what I feared, and how this all changed me. This subject of close encounters is one that would never go away, no matter where I went. In writing this book, it is not just an explanation for myself and the reader, but perhaps a healing mechanism for some who may have had similar experiences. I open my heart to those who suffer in silence. The pain of wanting to talk and the fear of being ridiculed can be overwhelming. So forward I will go to tell this story in my own raconteur way.

When we are very young, our understanding of the universe is limited to our short experiences. Yet as children we are more open to these experiences that may not make sense to adults. With an open mind, through time we may gain knowledge in both experiences and understanding of this UFO topic in a scientific way. We do so by asking questions and never fearing the questions nor the answers. By freeing the mind to possibilities that perhaps we are not alone in the universe. By understanding that perhaps one day, we can get there by travel to worlds far beyond ours and understand the worlds beyond the stars.

Chapter 1

My Warner Family and The 1835 Warner Homestead

Non Nobis Tantum Nati, We are not born for ourselves alone. The Warner Crest goes back to the days of the Wars of the Roses in England. This crest is so fitting that we must consider our journey of life as a gift and share that gift by helping others. Only by helping others can we have a successful life journey. Over the years we did so with honor, bravery, and unconditional love.

The Warners were a proud family here in America, going back to the 1600s in Massachusetts and early 1700s on Nantucket Island. The first Warner on record there, James Warner, was born in 1715. There is no record of his wife or parents. He was for sure a Warner, but possibly born on the wrong side of the blanket, something we may never know for sure. On October 29, 1775, his son, Gilbert Warner, married Sarah Ellis. Sarah was nineteen and Gilbert was twenty-three. The Ellis family were a well-established family on the Island and were related to the Coffins and Folgers. The wise Benjamin Franklin's grandparents were Folgers.

Gilbert, like his father before him, was a whaler, and like many on the island would take to the sea for his existence in this extreme and dangerous job. Then one day, the call to the sea changed, shortly after the young couple had married, from a way of life to the cause of defending Nantucket and very existence of life: the cause of the American Revolution.

Contrary to beliefs, being Quaker did not mean you would not fight, for when cornered to a cause, one would take arms. Fighting was never their first choice, but many took to the fight for Island and Country. Gilbert, his father-in-law, brother-in-law, and others headed out to defend America against all odds and face the mighty British Empire. Being local Nantucket whalers and having spent so much time at sea on these familiar waters was a major advantage.

The Nantucket boys had even discovered a stream that ran from the southeast to the northeast, now know as the Gulf Stream. With brave hearts and souls, this crew went to sea sailing and into history. However, the knowledge advantage of the northeast was not enough. The waters that brought them life went cold and rough and on one tragic day, all aboard their ship went down to the sea, taken in the fight for America's freedom.

Little did Gilbert know when he left his homeport on that fateful trip that his beloved Sarah was pregnant. By then, the island of Nantucket was under a blockade and they were being starved and the choice to leave or stay was now life-threatening. Not giving in to the British demands and with no practical choice, Sarah, along with other Quakers, escaped their island home. How sad that must have been to leave your home where you grew up, fell in love, married, became pregnant, then in one terrible day, lost everything. Gone forever, her father, brother, and husband. She and others made up their mind that they must leave Nantucket. Oh, the pain and sadness she felt must have been overwhelming, yet the family would carry on the hope of the pregnancy. In 1776, Sarah gave birth to a son, William, and the miracle of life continued.

With the help of other Quakers from Little Compton, Rhode Island, they all made their way to New York and to the safety of Hyde Park. The Quakers were brutalized back then, some even beaten and hanged for their religious beliefs. One generation after arriving in Hyde Park, Sarah's son William would grow up and marry into the historic Wilbur family, marring Elizabeth Wilbur from Little Compton, Rhode Island. Today, the family homestead in Little Compton is a historical site.

The Wilbur family's original name was Wildbore, but the name changed over the years. The Wilburs were one of seven families that had gone with Roger Williams after having been thrown out of the Massachusetts colony for becoming Quakers. In 1638, Samuel Wibore was the sixth signer of the Portsmouth Compact that established the first government in the world to allow and ensure its citizens civil and religious liberty. One hundred and thirty-eight years after this compact was signed, our nation declared another. The Portsmouth Compact was a prelude to the Declaration of Independence, which would forever change our democratic society. Freedom is as only as good as those willing to not judge others and let others have their own personal religious freedoms without being harassed or persecuted. Let no color of skin, no words of language, no beliefs in religion ever divide us.

William and Elizabeth's son Daniel, who was my great-great-grandfather, left Hyde Park in 1831 and came to Great Barrington, Massachusetts to become a cooper. After he learned his trade, he married his beloved Polly Smith. Then, on January 12, 1935, they moved to their new Warner Homestead farmhouse on a hill here in the western part of town locals call "Seekonk." In his large barn at the back of the house, he set up his shop making barrels. Not only did he make barrels, but the Warner family also had a farm, producing a large supply of produce for the town of Great Barrington. The barn eventually burned down, but I replaced it with a modest size barn-like art studio. Six generations later and we are still here at the family home. The homestead remains, but is now just a fraction of the once 180-acre farm.

Our family and homestead are listed in the book *Historic Homes and Institutions and Genealogical and Personal Memoirs of Berkshire County, Massachusetts*. History was well taught in our family, and what was not written in books was taught via the family raconteur of that particular generation. I guess this part of our family history with UFOs is going from the raconteur side to the print side; telling this story has been long overdue.

My generation of the Warner family consisted of six boys and one girl. This was sort of a typical large, Catholic baby boomer family of the '40s and '50s. Dad's great-grandparents became Methodists after not finding any Quaker meetings here. However, when Dad wanted to marry Mom, her Irish immigrant mother put down her demands: Fine, you can marry my daughter as long as you're Catholic! Love has a funny way of doing these things and religion was not going to stop Dad; of course, he converted. After World War II had ended, the baby boom was on in America and growing up then in a large family seemed normal to me. So many families I knew had six or seven children and there was always lots to do as far as activities.

The oldest child, my sister Judy, was born in 1948. She was eleven years older than me. By the time I was eleven she was ready to leave the nest! My earliest memory of Judy was that she was always very busy and had a nice boyfriend named Frank who was like an older brother to us. Frank was like part of the family then and often had a place at the dinner table. My parents were very fond of him, especially Mom!

After Judy, it was all boys from there and we came in rapid succession; Herby, born in 1949; Michael, born in 1952; Billy (also known as Rosco), born in 1953; followed by the identical twins John and Joe (also known as Bo), born in 1958. I was, as my father always called me, the caboose and was born in 1959.

Herby, being the oldest boy, influenced the personalities that we would develop, especially with his humor. He was always busting up and making his many friends double over in laughter. Most of my close interactions with Herby would come later as adults, though I do have fond memories from childhood, too.

My older siblings hung out and played together just because of the age difference. Not that as a group we didn't do things together, because we did plenty, but is was only natural that we were like two groups in one family. The twins and I would enjoy hours and hours of sandbox fun and a swing and slide that keep us very busy from spring to late fall. Looking at home movies, I see how happy we were just to climb a set of stairs to zip down that slide.

However, even while we played together there was a separation between the twins and myself. There is a special bond between twins that can never be denied and was quite fascinating to observe firsthand. These two identical brothers were inseparable in youth. In grade school, they would sometimes switch classes just to be funny. I was more like the observer with the twins, and when accepted, I was grateful to feel included in the time spent with them. Observing is a skill that takes patience and I learned along the way that this was necessary for survival on my journey in this large family.

Observation was the way with my older siblings as well; it was easier to observe than compete for attention. I will say, they gave us attention from time to time. Like when Michael and Billy would take us boys out fishing, especially the first day of the season. We would be so excited and off we would go with our push button Zebco poles and night crawlers, walking down to the Alford Brook. Michael would patiently help put the worms on the hooks. By the time we got home, the fishing creel was full of native trout ready for Ma to cook for dinner.

For the most part, as a group we got along well, as did most in the neighborhood. The neighborhood played endless games of baseball, football, and basketball. Games like hide-and-seek were also often played. Our hide-and-seek games went on for hours. Home base was safe as long as you didn't get caught before touching the base, which at our Warner Homestead and was the corner of the garage. You would get there and yell, Safe!

There were plenty of places to hide, but the prize for best hiding spot had to go to Bo. He went further than anyone of us had thought of when he climbed up onto the roof. Ma would not have been happy with that one! Whenever we would get a new idea to have fun, the idea usually included just a touch of danger. Danger was just another way to say be careful and pay attention. Sometimes we did pay attention and sometimes we didn't. Most importantly, for goodness sakes, don't tell Ma!

One summer day, Billy (Rosco) had bought a go-cart for twenty dollars from a neighbor named Ron. Oh, we were so excited when we saw that go-cart go! I couldn't wait to try the go-cart. The one problem with the go-cart was it had no brakes and when I say no breaks, I mean it, nada…none! It was a team effort to drive the go-cart that we so cleverly named Go-Cart. Simple enough name, but not so easy to operate.

The driver had to exit on one side as one or two held back Go-Cart while the next driver jumped in, and off you would go! We went for hours, going back and forth from the Warner Homestead to the Shaw's house next door. This lasted for a few years until just one missed transfer led to Go-Cart running away all alone. Unfortunately for us kids, Go-Cart found the pile of storm windows Dad had just put out to wash before putting them on for the upcoming winter. Go-Cart broke every one of them and that was pretty much the end of that fun! We were never bored and always had something to do, and with older brothers with great ideas, us younger boys were always waiting to see what they were up to next.

At one point, before my time, the Warner Homestead consisted of nearly 180 acres and two farms. By the time our generation came along much history and time passed. We were now down to a garden lot of two and a half acres and that was plenty for us. Still, there was a vast country setting back then with many farms and woods nearby. The house was barely big enough for us seven kids, Mom and Dad, Grandpa, and our beloved German shepherd, Ginger. To me however, the Warner Homestead was just fine.

The homestead had a large front porch that was used as entertainment and was one of the first bed-and-breakfasts in our county, dating back to when they first had the house in 1835 and entertainment was a family business. The bed-and-breakfast, named Shady Nook, was put on hold with our generation, as every room was full with us kids! Now the front porch was just a nice place to go and watch a good rainstorm or even be with Mom and Dad on a summer night listening to the crickets. The Berkshires were very rural, with part of our property on a dirt road that our great-great-grandparents had put in to go from one farm to a neighbor's farm. There were many dirt roads from when time was slower in America and life here in the Berkshires was truly like a reflection of many Norman Rockwell paintings.

Off the porch was the all important TV room, although we were only able to get three channels. That was all we knew and was fine enough; besides, there was the great outdoors of living in the country. The other important room, of course, was the dining room, which all eleven of us gathered around every night like clockwork. The railroad companies could have taken a lesson from Mom on how to keep everything running on time. Off the dining room was the library, or as Mom and Dad would say, our peace and quiet room. Grandpa loved that room, too, and in the corner was his special red chair reserved for him only. The hi-fi would play every Sunday with Ferlin Huskey for Grandpa and Louis Armstrong for Mom and Dad. Louis used to visit next door at the Nail home. They were in-laws to Mr. and Mrs. James Weldon Johnson. Johnson was one of our country's first civil rights leaders and they all became friends in those days with Dad, Grandpa, and Grandma. I can only imagine just how wonderful the experience must have been to sit on the porch and hear Satchmo play and sing.

I was always amazed by the amount of famous people who came through the Warner Homestead farmhouse doors. It was a simple 1835 farmhouse with a downstairs that had two bedrooms and a half bathroom, and an upstairs with a bathroom and four bedrooms. To this day we have made very few changes to the homestead and the feel is still very old-time New England.

There were so many kids in our neighborhood; not that there were that many families, but a small family back then was three and many had seven! The Shaw family was right next door and the Bean family was right across the street when I was a child. Back then, you didn't go to town if you were out of sugar or flour or even milk; you went next door and asked to borrow some. Mama needed a cup of sugar and you would come back with a cup of sugar. I called those my cup-of-sugar days, back when neighbors were neighbors.

The Bean family left the neighborhood early in my life, but the Shaw family remained through my high school years and they would forever become part of my life story and UFO story as well. They, too, had a large farmhouse, and their yard became the neighborhood baseball field. Over the years and time we went between the two houses so often that we beat down a dirt path that made riding our bicycles so much easier and safer to return after sunset.

Our old farm house was two and half miles outside of the town; a good walk to town, as Grandpa would say. Our neighborhood was called Seekonk and at one point, long before me, the Seekonk School was across the street from us, along with a grist mill and a gin mill. Eventually they were torn down or burned.

The story on our barn was that it burned because of a moonshine incident. They made moonshine up in the hills and then had parties at the Warner barn. The barn and the moonshine were victims of an arsonist. My Uncle Gil reluctantly told me the story as the next raconteur of the family. Seems the distillery they had was busted up and they blamed Uncle Gil, so it was payback.

In front of where the old barn was, there was a clay tennis court for the guests to use. In time, the courts disappeared and turned to grass. This was our perfect place to play and have baseball catches, and play football and even soccer. I think we must have been some of the first around here to play soccer. We still call that flat area the tennis court to this day, though now it's a tennis hill thanks to a new modern septic system! Our homestead's name, Shady Nook, was because of all the maple trees on the property that were planted by the different generations, still providing wonderful shade all these years later.

Now, if the weather was good, we kids went outside; if the weather wasn't so good, we went outside anyways. Perhaps if there was a storm we didn't, but that was the exception. Our time was spent playing down on the Alford Brook or in the family garden. The garden was necessary for a healthy part of our provisions. Weeding was taught at an early age and the garden was kept immaculate and produced an amazing amount of green beans, yellow beans, asparagus, tomatoes, and other vegetables. We never had to buy vegetables or fruit. By season's end, all those provisions were in the freezer or the old mason jars.

I wasn't too big on vegetable picking, but loved going after strawberries and blueberries. We would go to different places to pick and looked forward to the annual trip. Us kids sampled plenty while picking, and I'm sure the stains on our faces gave us away.

Back home, Mom would prepare and freeze the berries and put them in a special section of the freezer where they would stay till winter or special deserts. Oh, that fruit we gathered in the summer would come out nearly every Sunday. The frozen fruit would thaw on the old cast-iron radiator and once in a while I would sneak a sample when no one was looking. In the depth of a cold New England winter, berries now in the form of pie or strawberry short cake with homemade whipped cream made a wonderful dessert.

Every Sunday, we all went to Catholic church at 7 AM, followed by picking up the Sunday newspaper. Once home, Mom and Dad had peace and quiet in the library and us kids got to watch TV. If we did want to read the Sunday funnies, we had to keep the noise down. Once the reading was finished, the hi-fi went on. As if it was a signal, roast beef dinner would be served be at 12:10. Our clock was always ten minutes fast to keep us on time. My goodness, Mom was a fine cook! We all pitched in to help in any way asked. The effort was a group one on team Warner.

Mom and Dad worked so hard to raise us kids. I have no idea how they worked so hard just to make a better life for us. Mom worked all day at home keeping up with cooking, cleaning, and running a household. She was truly an amazing woman. So often we would have a dozen for dinner, and stretching a budget and having us all satisfied was no easy task. Her Irish mother's influence of potatoes and vegetables and meat were a constant favorite.

After dinner and clean up, us youngest went to bed. Mom would read us a story and each of us said our prayers, called Goodnight God. We went to sleep and then Mom would take a nap before going to work as a nurse on the 11 PM-7 AM shift at our local Fairview Hospital. To this day, I don't know how she worked the way she did. The woman hardly slept a wink in my lifetime. Dad worked just as hard and had a lawn service along with his full-time job. All this to keep us housed, fed, and happy, something I appreciate to this day. Dad worked a few towns away as a paper inspector. He would get home after working eight hours then would go back with my Mom to mow those lawns in the summer to make extra money. The good part of their jobs was vacations in the summer. I never thought about who they got to do their lawn service jobs when we went away, but as a kid, you don't think in those terms.

One of the reasons they worked so hard was to take a vacation to their favorite lake. They had loved lakes ever since they first got married back in 1946 and honeymooned on Lake George, New York. Now as a married couple, they went a bit farther north to Lake Champlain, near a town called Port Henry. Lake Champlain was a special place for all of us, but for me it was like a bond with nature and more. Little did I know at the time how this would affect me as the years passed.

In Port Henry, we stayed down on a cabin right on the water. The cabin I remember the most was called the Four Leaf Clover because it had one main living area and four big rooms off the main area. The main area had wonderful and typical Adirondack furniture, and of course an out-of-tune piano. I think a lot of cabins in the North Country had them as entertainment, and being in an isolated area, this was a plus for renters. What memories we had singing around that piano.

Now, to get down to the the property where the Four Leaf Clover was, you had to go down one of the steepest roads one could imagine. OK, so how steep, you ask? At the top of the road you had to start blasting your car horn so that you let someone know you were coming down, for no two cars could ever meet. Not sure what they would do if they had! Once down, you stopped at the bottom then listened intently before crossing the D&H railroad tracks. Once across the D&H, you had arrived at the lake.

The property, which had about seven cabins and a wonderful sandy beach, was owned by a couple named Blonde and Eva. Blonde was a happy fellow and when he smiled you could see his gold tooth. He had a big belly and was red in the face, perhaps from a bit too much of that homemade grappa drink. Of course his hair, once blond, now was showing some grey. I remember thinking at the time that perhaps he was related to Santa. His wife, Eva, I thought might be related to our neighbor Irene Shaw, who we called Gram. She always seemed to have an apron on and perhaps she was often cooking for guests, but whatever the reason, I always felt the kindness of that couple, even at a young age.

We loved the place at Port Henry, as Blonde made a great playground for kids, complete with slides, swings, and a sandbox. Like back home in Great Barrington, there were lots of kids. Up by his workshop, he had a soda box with ice, and here at Port Henry, I had my first Mountain Dew. For many years, I thought Blonde and Eva made the Mountain Dew themselves. Blonde didn't make Mountain Dew, but he sure did make that grappa moonshine. Dad and his friend called Papa Nick had some, but Ma and Emily (Papa Nick's wife) declined!

Along with the playground, they provided renters with a huge inflatable navy surplus raft that Blonde turned over and had anchored off his well-manicured, sandy beach. This was a perfect raft for all to enjoy. I remember being brought out to the raft the first time and sitting in the middle, going up and down with the Lake Champlain waves. From the beach to the playground, us kids played all day long. Right after supper we could sit out on flat rocky area in front of the camp, and it was here that I first got the feeling of something unexplainable. The feeling was only when I sat by the water looking to the north and east across Lake Champlain. Something was calling to me, to my mind in a way that words were not needed. At the time I did not understand what was happening or even where this was coming from, but just that it was.

Now as a child, I was developing mental telepathy, but with whom? Even at a young age I said nothing to anyone about this. Besides, really, who would believe that I was communicating to some far off and distant beings? Of course, at the time I was not even sure if what I was hearing was real, but in time I would be shown that indeed it was. Often, I found myself thinking of conversing with the mind rather that using words. No one really asked when I was having quiet moments what I was thinking or why I was quiet, but for me they were not quiet moments at all. In my mind, there was a voice of a little girl and as I grew, so did she. I was learning mental telepathy without knowing where it was coming from. I can see all the psychologists trying to analyze this away. However, some things just can not be explained away and only make sense over time and with events.

Not that this was an everyday occurrence, but from time to time the telepathy did happen. I began to accept this strange ability, but always wondered and came back to the same question: Why me? After much thinking, I came to understand the why was not important and I felt comfortable in knowing who I was.

Chapter 2
Bumps, Bruises, and Close Calls

I remember the day like it was yesterday. We had just gotten back home from the lake. Both Grandpa and Ginger greeted us like we had been gone for months, but I am sure it was only two weeks at most. All my toys were in their places, just where I had left them. My toy truck parked in the sandbox was waiting for action, my sandbox road that led to my house made with sticks and mud. I had spent hour after hour of both imagination and time to perfect this childhood skill of sandbox building. I kept my blue toy truck right up next to the large maple tree. Just past the sandbox was our slide that we used on a daily basis. Alternating between the two places, the sandbox and slide, we went like a flowing, meandering creek, never making any sense; we just went from one to the other.

The sandbox was perfect, with the shade of the maple tree, a gift planted years and years ago by my great-grandfather, Henry C. Warner. Henry was a historical writer in his day, writing for newspapers and periodicals from Springfield, Massachusetts to New York City and recording the history of Berkshire County, Massachusetts. He was a proud member of the Berkshire County Historical Association and the residence of this organization was the home and now museum of the famous writer Herman Melville. Grandpa would talk about him often, telling stories of the past. Hearing the same stories over and over, I was being groomed as the future raconteur of the Warner family. I suppose this book will be the ultimate raconteur story from the homestead, one I wish Grandpa could have read.

Drifting back in time to my first bad bump and bruise: I never had any recollection of the matter, but do remember first being told of the incident. Now see, my Dad was always looking out for us kids because he had already hit my older brother, Michael, and now that there were three more of us, Dad had to be extra careful. The twins, Bo and John, were so active that his eyes must be trained like a papa eagle keeping track of his wild bunch. Apparently, he was not careful enough and although he did see where twins were, he somehow forgot to look for his caboose. As he went to back out of the dirt driveway, I was hit with the family station wagon. I was just two years old when this happened.

I was told I moved just enough not to have the wheels hit me, but still was hit in the head by the bumper and dragged until Dad stopped, as he heard everyone screaming. It was all a bit too late, as I was now trapped under the car. Mom now heard Dad screaming to call the police, call the fire department, call for an ambulance: Oh my God, I ran over Tommy. I can't imagine the pain, fear, and panic he must have been going through at that moment.

Mom, of course was a bit more calm than Dad, perhaps because she was a nurse or perhaps she was just plain calm, a skill I paid attention to that has served me well my entire life. Rapidly, half the neighborhood ran to the homestead to see if they could help, from the Shaw family to the Bean family and more. By now, Mom was laying on the ground, reaching for her two-year-old baby boy. Years later, she told me how she slowly pulled me away and handed me off to a young neighbor, Delphine Bean, who was the first to hold my nearly lifeless body. Delphine thought I was gone, but I came to rather quickly. I am sure I let out a good cry on that one, a cry Delphine and everyone else there was happy to hear, especially Dad. The poor man must have been a wreck. I had a bad burn from the muffler and a minor concussion. But then again, Mom called everything minor!

Not only had I had this close call, but years later I found out Mom had a heart attack after I had been conceived. I knew this because the time of year she had her attack was in 1958 during the strawberry picking season and the fact I was full-term baby born nine months later. Mom was a legendary tough Irish woman, something all our friends would come to learn in time. She was tough, strong, and oh dear Lord, she deserved sainthood raising all us Warner boys.

Not long after I was born, I had scarlet fever and had to be hospitalized in isolation. This was in the spring of 1959, and apparently the doctor was being a bit rough with me and I was crying. Mom announced that she was a nurse and would be staying with me. At first the doctor objected, but there was no stopping Ma. Dad asked, Why are you being so mean to my son? According to Dad, the doctor had words with both of my parents and said he was off for the weekend to go fishing up on Lake Champlain. Dad said, Be careful of storms this weekend. The doctor sarcastically replied, I know what I am doing. That was his last fishing trip; while out fishing, his boat was struck by lightning and he was instantly killed.

Mom always said I had some sort of Irish angel protection around me. Of course, they must have been Irish; Nana would not have it any other way! Being raised Catholic, and the fact my mom's mom, who we called Nana, was born in Ireland, she had every right to think that. I would take years to believe in the possibility of angels, but in time that, too, would change. Yes, all too often time has a way of doing that, showing us that all things are possible.

Oh with us boys, Ma would have both the candles and novena prayers going nonstop. At night after I said my prayers, I would say them again, as I had difficulty sleeping so often, even though I slept in the same room as Bo and John. They had bunkbeds way over on the opposite side of the room. Back then that felt like ten miles away from me and my bed, which was in the coldest part of the house in the northwest corner. I think it was possible it could snow in that part of our room in the winter, or at least it felt that way.

I would ask to sleep with one of them, but the answer was always no, and so me and my teddy bear would go off to Grandpa's room, where he always had room for his Little Tom. By morning I would be up with the safe sunrise. Slumber would never be easy and it was years before I learned to sleep well.

Often, Grandpa would not say much, but I always felt I knew what he was thinking. I would wave goodbye to him before he would announce he was walking to town. My goodness, could that man walk. Every day, even when old, he would walk the two and a half miles to town and back again. A woman once told the story of how he drove about a hundred yards in an attempt to learn the art of driving the automobile. He stopped and told the woman, No, thank you, I will wait till the world comes to its senses and brings back the reliable horse and buggy. Well that hasn't happened yet, Grandpa!

Once while visiting my Uncle Gil in Virginia, he found out that there was going to be a parade with President Eisenhower, and good Lord, he walked seven miles to see the president. I think about his walk, and it still blows my mind that he walked so far. He walked the two and half miles from Seekonk to Great Barrington and back at least once a day unless there was a storm. When Grandpa got back, he would often give out candies, and while others shared he would give me my own candy bar. I was fine with that too. Back then a Hershey Bar was a Hershey Bar!

The year was 1963, and being a big four-year-old, I was now allowed to play outside by myself. For some reason, the only ones home this particular day were Grandpa and me. I asked to go out side to play in the sandbox and I got the answer, OK, Little Tom. The funny thing about traumatic events is the clarity with which every detail is etched into your memory, and this was going to be one of those days. I was by the maple tree and a car went by slowly, which in those days was nothing unusual. Mrs. Hendricks, a nearby neighbor, drove by at approximately seven miles per hour, and she always smiled and waved. However, this car that went by was different, as they went around the block a second time and pointed at me; I felt uneasy right away.

I will never forget what they looked like; at the time, I thought they looked very strange to me. Today, I even wonder if they were human-alien hybrids. There were three young men and three young women, and they looked to be in their early twenties. The guys had typical short hair and were very fair, not as blond as me, but very light. The young ladies were all blonde. I just knew something was not right when they looked at me going by the first time. Then I saw them drive around our country block. We live up on a hill, so you could see a car going back around. They passed a second time, going even more slowly than the first time, and stopped just past the Shaw's.

I looked up, and the first thing I saw was a bush across the road; I bolted into the bush and laid on the ground, crouched like a scared rabbit. I could hear my heartbeat and feared that they would hear the beating too. I was so scared I was trembling. Then the car, which was a dark blue convertible, backed up and stopped right by me. I thought I was well hidden, but was not overly confident. These six young adults in the car were trying to lure me out from my hiding. Was this because I was a towhead blond or something else that I would never know for sure? They started to call for me as I continued to tremble even more in the bush. First the driver, then the woman next to him called out, Come out little boy, we have some candy for you! I wasn't tempted by their call, not even for candy and trust me, I loved candy!

At this very moment, I knew I could not scream for Grandpa, who was in the house, nor could I run as I would have been easily taken. I thought back to that place on Lake Champlain and a voice spoke to me in my mind. The voice was a girl and she said, Call to your Grandpa with your mind, but your mind only. Scream for him in your mind. So I did. In my mind I screamed, Grandpa, HELP! I heard the driver say, He has to be near here, and at that moment, Grandpa came out of the homestead with his rifle and took aim at the car. Driver, he yelled, I am a sharpshooter for the New York National Guard. If this car moves, you are dead. I want my grandson, NOW!

This is when I said, I'm here, Grandpa, and came out. Grandpa went over to the car with his rifle. I watched him as he looked at them and it was as if he had seen a ghost. He threatened them to not come back again, then let them go.

Yes, I was surprised that he let them go. He told me not to worry and that they wouldn't come back, but after looking at them, Grandpa looked scared himself; that was the only time I ever saw fear in my grandpa's eyes. We are not going to talk about this with anyone, Little Tommy, he said. OK, Grandpa, I replied, and I never did, till now.

Grandpa made me stay in the rest of the time, and the slide and sandbox were moved the next day up to the back of our property, away from the road. Grandpa said he heard me call to him, but I never said how I actually called to him; somehow, I think he knew it was all mental telepathy, the ability to talk from mind to mind without words actually being spoken. I did not have a good feeling about what had happened, and the situation made me wonder what they wanted with me. It was so much for a little four-year-old fellow to take in, and I was so happy to have Grandpa, who was one heck of a shot. I know had that car moved, Grandpa would have shot for sure, and I know they knew that as well. I was a target, but why and for whom I will never know. Had they taken me, they would have been the target, and Grandpa never missed.

Grandpa Warner was in the New York National Guard since the young age of fifteen. He was with the New York National Guard 71st division in the Spanish-American War of 1898 and the First World War as well. He never talked much about war and his service, but rather what was good in life. He was a man of action with his words and this was his way of life. I took in every word he had to say, for when he did speak he made every word count. He was brave and heroic and very well-respected in our town. When we had our town bicentennial here in Great Barrington, our family, with Grandpa, led off the celebration. Those pictures, a moment in town history, were such a special way to see my Grandpa from all those yeas ago.

Like so many Americans, on November 22, 1963, our world felt as though it had come to a stop. President Kennedy was dead. I heard it myself right on our TV. Our president had been assassinated. I heard Mom ask, How could anyone shoot our president? I was but a child, but I could feel the devastation in my parents' voices. Everyone was both shocked and saddened. Thanksgiving felt so somber that year as Grandpa said grace and looked at me and said, Amen, Little Tom. The Macy's Thanksgiving Day Parade, which they had considered cancelling, went on as a part of healing, and in time America would heal as well. Dad stated that Santa was in the parade and all felt OK again and safe in the Warner Homestead. Danger was just a natural part of my life and always present and concerning.

New Year's 1964 came, and I was told Grandpa was going to Florida for the winter. Grandpa must have been one of the first snowbirds I had ever known! The train would take him from Great Barrington to New York, then on to Miami, Florida. I cried to myself all the way home. On my fifth birthday, in March, I got a card from Grandpa. Mom said he would be home before we knew it. Sure enough, the long New England winter of nor'easters would let go to the warmth of the spring sun. The melting snow and the rebirth of spring was here. I sit here writing my autobiography all these years later in the exact spot in our library where Grandpa's red chair was and I can't help but to remember him and the aura of kindness that surrounded him.

That summer, Grandpa had what they called a mild stroke, and he no longer could walk to town and had to accept rides. I have a vague memory of taking a short walk with Grandpa while my Mom was shopping at the old A&P grocery store. The one thing that left an ever-lasting impression was how many people always greeted Grandpa with a, Hello, Mr. Warner, or, Hello, Will. He was so revered in those days gone by in our Berkshire town.

That summer, before we went on vacation to Lake Champlain, Grandpa sat me down and told me a scary story about a guy down the road who had hung himself and that the rope was buried in a well, and that I should never go near it. I was to understand the dangers that could get into people. He had never told me a scary story before, so I listened and promised I would never go near the well just down the lane. Years later, I found that the story was true and I stayed away from that well until one day, I felt compelled to go there to make peace.

Many years would pass before I heard the entire story. The story started with Grandpa's sister Lottie, who at the young age of sixteen fell in love with a boy down the lane named Dwight Burgett. She and the boy made love and, of course, you guessed it, she became pregnant, and young Dwight and Lottie wanted to wed. His tyrannical mother, Mary, was having nothing to do with those Warners, and forbid his son to marry young Lottie. Her heart was broken to pieces by that woman.

My great-grandparents must have been furious with the Burgett family. Lottie was so devastated that she moved to the family residence in New York. Dwight was so devastated that he attempted to kill himself.

He survived the attempt, but was blinded by his gunshot injury. His mother now demanded that his brother produce a son to carry on their family name. Too bad she didn't let the young couple marry, as the child Lottie and Dwight produced was a son. Lottie met a young man and they married. Her husband adopted the young baby. The story does not end there, because Dwight's brother Leon, after having all girls, was devastated not to give a son. One hot summer day, Grandpa went down the lane to the Bergett barn to return some tools he had borrowed. Poor Grandpa opened the barn door just as Leon jumped and hung himself, his dead body nearly hitting Grandpa as it went swinging by. Grandpa cut him down and ran for help. The entire neighborhood was in shock for years after that terrible day. I made peace with that family and am in contact with my dear cousin Nancy, who came to our homestead to hear the story. I prayed for Leon and his brother who had to bear the burden of his mother's judgmental ways.

It is all too common to find those who judge that someone is not good enough based on some fake crazy social notion. I came to learn this in my teens and early adulthood and the story told by Grandpa was for me to understand years later. He was wise, knowing he would be gone, yet still comforting me with his raconteur storytelling that would give me lessons and comfort on my life journey. I think he knew my sensitivity was the Achilles' heel to my vulnerable heart and soul. I went to that well and made peace and let Leon know that. After my visit to pray there, all was fine and peace was restored.

Back at the lake, these intense feelings of mental telepathy continued to grow as I often would look out on the lake to the north and to the east. Such a strange feeling, the thought of far away contacts, but over time I just accepted this ability. It was like I had a friend in my mind if needed, and she was real. Not real in a physical sense, but she was out there somewhere. By now, I was being raised a Catholic and I just figured she must be some sort of angel, and I was fine with that. As if that wasn't interesting enough, that was the first year I was told of a legend of a lake monster at Lake Champlain. A lake monster that years later, with the help of the famous great cartoon artist Sid Couchey, would be named Champy.

Dad took me for a walk down a few houses away from our Four Leaf to visit an older couple, Dot and Frank, who had a small cabin. They had bought the cabin from Blonde and were there all summer long. They were in their Adirondack rocking chairs and greeted us warmly. Dot made us a fancy bologna sandwich with a Mountain Dew. I loved having a Mountain Dew, as we never had that back home in Massachusetts. So there we were, and Dot says, Ain't that right, Frank?

What's that, Dot?

You know, the lake monster that we saw this spring when we first got up here.

Yup, that's right, Dot. Must have been well over twenty feet or more, Frank responded. My eyes must have opened up like silver dollars, hearing that for the first time, the story of the Lake Champlain Monster. Got to love that Lake Champlain, never a dull moment around campfires and we had plenty of both that summer vacation.

The Lake taught me to listen to nature. I remember going down to the lake shore to check on the boats with Dad. The weather appeared perfect, but the lake was saying something different to me. Dad, I said, there's going to be a storm.

Ya think so, son? Why?

I don't know why, I just see waves coming.

Before night fell, I was right and Dad must have listened to me, because I heard him saying to Mom not to worry, and that he had tied the boats up well. We all watched the storm safely from the Four Leaf Clover, while outside the lake roared. I went to sleep that night to the rhythm of those waves upon the rocks. Before long, our stay at Lake Champlain was over and soon Labor Day would conclude the story of summer.

When we got back from the lake, I remember Grandpa was now resting more than ever and sometimes he even took naps during the day. One night, I woke up with a start like someone had touched me. Right away, I went straight to Grandpa's room. Grandpa, something scared me. Can I sleep with you?

Climb over, Little Tom, came the answer. So me and my Teddy did, and I went fast asleep.

I woke up the next morning and I was in my own bed and in different pajamas. Mom came into the room and I could tell something was wrong. She said Michael and Billy were going to take us for a walk around the block, all this before breakfast. We took our time and I still was confused why were going for a walk before breakfast. Ma always made us breakfast before we did anything, but not on this day. My older brothers paying attention to us was enough to get us to go. We took our time walking around the block and when we got back we were told the news: Grandpa died during the night. He has gone to heaven. I was in his arms when he died, something I knew, but Mom and Dad waited years to tell me. I had lost my Grandpa, my hero.

Two weeks later, on a Sunday, I was the last to to run out to the car for church. There in the hall was an image of Grandpa. He waved to me, told me to do good, and said he had to leave now. His image went right into the wall. I just stared and opened the closet door but he was gone. With that I ran so fast outside with an expression on my face of pure fright. Mom asked right away what was wrong and I told her. She didn't say a word but prayed a little longer before mass. My hero now was gone to heaven, I thought. I had to learn to be brave now. That day in church I prayed that I would learn be brave and strong like Grandpa.

My fifth year was almost my last year alive. Winter had settled in early in New England with lots of cold and snow. I don't know whose idea it was to take the big toboggan to the Shaw farm down the road. I think this was the only time I ever rode the toboggan. I am sure the toboggan wasn't that big, but to a five-year-old, it was large enough! The Shaw family who owned the farm were not related to the Shaw family who lived right next door, but at the time I had just assumed they were. In the back of Farmer Shaw's property was a steep, and I mean steep, hill. We went down that hill so fast and by the time we stopped, we were down by the Alford Brook that ran through their property.

The brook was all covered with ice as we stood on the edge. All of us were there: Bo, John, Michael, Billy, and myself. When Billy said, It's OK, you can walk out farther, I did. Oh sure, send the youngest! Well, that was not a good idea, not a good idea at all. In an instant the ice gave way beneath my feet and I plunged into the ice-cold Alford Brook.

I went all the way under the water and came up taking in a deep breath of air. Oh, that ice-cold Alford Brook water instantly took my breath away. The water was so cold and felt more like a burn to me. Then, in that moment time slowed to a crawl and went into slow motion. Here I was, only five years old, and time was in slow motion as I tried to survive. Somehow, I knew that and right away, I heard that angel-like voice say, Grab the ice above, and so I did. Do not let go till they pull you out, came the next instruction. I was somehow calm in this moment as I looked down the brook at death. There was a space of about ten inches between the flowing water and ice that would have trapped and drowned me. These catacombs of nature looked both beautiful and terrifying at the same time. I knew if I let go I would die, so naturally, letting go was not an option. The water was so quiet under the ice and my body hurt so bad. The ice-cold water was babbling beneath the ice so peacefully while the cold was squeezing the air out of me. I was having trouble getting air in, as my breathing hurt so much and the burning feeling intensified. Finally I felt the grip of two hands on my wrists and heard the call, Pull! Out I came. Michael was the first to react, and he and Billy both put me on the toboggan and they pulled like crazy, rushing to get me home. Ma must have seen the boys rushing up the hill as she was giving them her infamous look that said, What have you done? Oh, my God, what happened? Take him to the upstairs bathroom right now, I remember her saying.

Oh, I could tell by her voice she was so upset with my older brothers. You're suppose to be watching them, she snarled. Mom's snarl was even a bit more frightful than the look and I actually felt sorry for them at that moment. I thought, Oh boy, they are never taking me anywhere after this. Thankfully, they eventually would.

By the time we got upstairs, Mom was more happy that I was still alive. Mom, being a nurse, took over and cut off my frozen clothes that were stuck to my body. The warm bath, now drawn, awaited me. The warm water hurt and was too hot. I protested, but in her reassuring mommy voice, she said, No, Tommy, you are too cold. It will be OK, Mommy will feel it first. After a while, my body got used to the temperature and warmed up slowly. Dried off and in the comfort of my PJs, I walked down to a loving pat on the head from my brothers. That experience was way too close a call for anyone.

The only thing I remember after that was being on the couch with lots of blankets and having my favorite homemade hot cocoa and toast. When everyone left and my siblings could not see me, I began to cry uncontrollably. I felt confused because it was like I knew of the danger, and yet I still went and faced a danger to prove I was brave, not only to myself but also to my brothers. I wanted to be accepted by them on equal terms. Whatever the reason, this close call made me cry. All this before my sixth birthday. So many bumps, bruises, and close calls.

Chapter 3

Sports, Art, and Spiritual Beginnings

All my brothers played baseball, but the idea of playing baseball just did not appeal to me, mostly because I was lousy at catching a ball that was as hard as a rock. My older brothers, Michael and Billy, had already played minor league and little league by the time us younger boys were that age to play. When it came time for me to play minor league, I said a polite, No, thank you! The twins, Bo and John, played very well and I could see how proud my parents were of them at games. I admired how they played sports without any fear and wondered how to achieve the edge they had so naturally. There was one thing in sports I was good at, and that was running. I really had some wheels as a child and I loved that I could run fast, but that still didn't help me catch a baseball.

They loved the game and I wanted to as well because they all did. My fear of a hard object overruled me trying at that time. Although there were no youth teams, my game was soccer. I was happy just to run around with that soccer ball, kicking and running whenever I could. Every day, I used to practice a trick to pick the ball up with my foot. I don't know how many years it took before I could, but when I did there was no turning back. Years later, I had the nickname Soccer Tom. I was so happy in grade school when they played kickball or soccer in gym because I did so well at these games.

Even in a social setting, it was hard to live up to my older brothers; they were outgoing and bold and I was quiet and shy. Oh sure, I could talk, but I had a quiet part of me that no one would understand. The quiet part of me was the beginning of my spiritual side. This was etched in my belief that there was something else out in the world far beyond our own earth. Mom wanted to believe it was because we were being raised Catholic. In one picture Dad took of me for first communion, there was a shadow of a sign of a cross on my chest that could not be explained. To this day, I have no idea and will say that was very strange.

This spiritualness I felt came from the stars above me, the mountains and hills that I climbed, the water in streams and lakes that we enjoyed and played in and the trees we hid behind to the garden where we grew our vegetables; It all meant so much to me. I felt my spiritualness, and even at a young age felt there were two forces in the world. There was a good force and a bad force. The good force would try and help me on my life journey and the bad force would try to hurt me. How is it that by six years old I came so close to death so many times or would see such evil as almost being kidnapped? At the same time this was so trivialized in my family, perhaps because everyone was in a battle for attention and in this way we all got a little lost from time to time.

Down the hill from us was a neighbor's house where my parents were caretakers. At the back of the property was a cabin where we ventured out to cross a birch bridge over a small tributary that flowed into the Alford Brook. The cabin sat up on the hill and wasn't just any cabin, but a historical cabin that belonged to James Weldon Johnson, the civil rights leader. He wrote the famous *God's Trombones* in this cabin. This property was the inspiration of so many of his works including one of his famous writings "Lift Every Voice and Sing," which became the Negro National Anthem.

Even at a young age, we were told who Johnson was. James was the first field secretary of the NAACP. His anthem is one of the most cherished songs of the civil rights movement. James was a man of diplomacy and action, working on anti-lynching legislation. I felt his spirit there, when years later as a poet and artist I would be honored to receive the Legacy Award by the James Weldon Johnson Literary Foundation for stellar contributions to Literature and the Arts. On the award was a quote by Johnson: "The final measure of greatness of all peoples is the amount and standard of the literature and art they have produced." I was told by the director of the James Weldon Johnson Literary Foundation in her speech that the last time the award was given was to civil rights leader Vernon Jordan. Tears filled my eyes as I was overcome with emotion when my name was called up to receive the award. I was at a loss for words but managed a short speech just the same.

James and his wife, Grace Nail Johnson, were friends of Grandpa and Grandma Warner. Grandpa helped them build their house on the famous Five Acres property. On June 26, 1938, James was tragically killed in a car accident in Wiscasset, Maine. Mrs. Johnson survived, and Mom and Dad remained close friends with Mrs. Johnson. Naturally, after Five Acres was sold, they became the caretakers. I was happy to just go out to the cabin that had a spiritual feel. Could a location be a spiritual destination? There was and is a very unusual feel to this area to this day. In conversations, I have had people tell me they come to this area looking for paranormal activity, and look to the skies for UFOs.

One time at the cabin after Bo, John, and I went inside and had a good look around, the twins got bored and wanted to leave. I wanted to stay and listen to the brook. John had a great idea to play by a log and jump off it. That sounded good at the moment but oh, that was a bad idea. The log was a the home to a large nest of yellow jackets. Bo was always first to give the command, RUN, bees! and we were off. Oh, run we did, right to Ma, screaming, Bees, bees! Wherever Bo ran, I ran, and when he ran all the way home, I was right behind him. I am not even sure

John got a single sting, but Bo and I got nailed at least six times. So much for wanting to hang out with the twins. I thought for years how the bees must be protecting the cabin. Today the process is underway to preserve the historic cabin by the neighbors Jill and Rufus Jones, who bought the famed property and formed the James Weldon Johnson Foundation to advance the Johnson's legacy. Luckily for all, the bees had moved on!

No matter what game we played, I was never comfortable and felt like the older kids had an edge, because they did. They learned to ride a bike before me, play baseball before me, and because the twins and I were only thirteen months apart, I felt like we were the same age. By now, the easiest way for me to avoid some of the sports I was trying to avoid was to go next door to the Shaw's and play. Debbie was older than me, but there was one thing Debbie loved to do that I did as well, and that was color. I loved to color and Debbie had the sixty-four Crayola set; before long, I did as well. Page after page we would color. She would critique my work in such a kind way and always pointed out to try and stay in the lines. I had a tough time doing this but worked hard at my early art form of coloring. Because I was a natural lefty forced to use my right hand, I had to concentrate and I enjoyed this immensely. I am naturally quicker and have more strength to this day on my left side, but the concentration helped so much in my preparation to become a watercolor artist years and years later. I will always be grateful to Debbie and to her sister, Jane, who treated me with such kindness and never put me down for things I did not want do. That which was considered a weakneses turned out to be a strength. I did not realize how much the time I spent with Deb helped me and gave me the roots needed to be drawn to the arts. We would spend hour after hour doing art just with crayons. I still have one piece I did when I was just four years old.

There was never any competition for anything. If we wanted to watch TV, we just watched, and if not, we colored or played board games, but never once did I feel like I had to win. I really enjoyed Deb's friendship, even though she was a few years older than me. Not only Deb, but often her sister, Jane, was usually around playing cards with her grandmother, who we all called Gram. She was a fixture in the neighborhood and was so well-respected and loved by every person who met her. Gram always made sure you felt welcomed and never went away hungry.

In those early years, even the Shaws loved playing sports, so every once in awhile I would too, but avoided any action at every cost. A baseball hit my way was an easy hit, as I let it go by and and would just run after it. It's called catch, not fetch Tommy! the kids would call. But running was something I could do well and so I did! As young kids, we were pretty typical of the 1960s, riding bikes and doing the kind of things most American kids did. When I was nine, I wanted to fit in and I was ready to give this baseball game and little league a go. I sucked; no, really, I sucked at baseball and although I had no business on a field, when picking teams they took me anyways. Truth was, they wanted the star Warner twins and I was the polite part of a package deal. That was a bonus of being the youngest behind the athletic twins.

They started and played and I sat and watched. The coach said for me to watch and maybe one day I would learn to play. I was so humiliated. Some kid on the bench asked if I want to have a catch, which was better than sitting on the bench. The sun was in my eyes and I said that we had to move.

Right then, he threw the ball and it hit me right in the mouth. I screamed in pain so loud that Bo heard me in the outfield as blood was pouring out of my mouth. The coach had me rinse out my mouth with water and luckily that was the last inning. I looked for Dad to pick us up but he did not show up. For some reason my parents thought we had a ride home but we didn't. Every tooth in my mouth was loose and I was still bleeding. The three of us walked the three miles home. Both Bo and John were so good to me as they could see the pain and the fear in my face, thinking I would lose my teeth. Bo kept on saying it would be all right, reminding me before we knew it we would be going up to the new place on Lake Champlain. All the way home I visualized healing, but moaned every step of the way. We arrived at the house just as Mom and Dad got home. Mom, Tommy's hurt real bad, my brothers explained. The first few days after that I could only have liquids and consumed lots of Jello. Mom bought me new crayons and a few coloring books but I was saving them for going to a new place on Lake Champlain. In a few weeks time, my teeth began to tighten and there was less pain every day. Soon we would be going to my beloved Lake Champlain to a new place Mom and Dad found to rent.

I remember pulling onto Willsboro Point for the first time. The lake was nearly six miles wide here and on some days you could not see the other side. We arrived at the cabin and all rushed down to see the lake and get our first impressions. The first thing I felt was the summer breeze and I heard the repeating waves that, on this day, were pretty choppy. This was even a bit intimidating for the first time. The Willsboro location on the lake was much bigger than down in Port Henry. The cabin we were renting was owned by the Seyfarth-Cowern Family and I am close friends with the family to this day.

The cabin had two floors with an upstairs porch and a downstairs porch. My older brothers took the downstairs porch, leaving two bedrooms for the twins and my parents, and I had the upstairs porch. The cot I had was not the most comfortable, but hearing the waves every night rocked me to sleep. If that was not enough to put one into a deep sleep, Dad listed to his music on WJOY out of Burlington that could even put a colicky baby into deep slumber.

Every evening the the lights of Burlington, Vermont, came on like clockwork and we would sit on our sandy beach and watch them appear one by one. On many nights, the lake would get as calm as glass and you could listen to the cries of the far off gulls and the ever so subtle clanging of a nearby sailboat mast. We would sit around the campfire building s'mores and memories as we would point out a distant boat with a reflection of port or starboard light.

We would sing songs, but Dad would always finish with his famous family song of "Show Me The Way To Go Home." I had found my spiritual home right here on these shores. This was more than a place. The lake called out to me as did the night sky. The water, the distant mountains, the wildlife of calling loons and seagulls were just part of the picture. Far more than all this, I felt something as the campfire glowed and the night sky called to my very soul and I wondered.

This 120-mile long Lake Champlain once was home to powerful Indigenous nations. The Mohawk tribe called Willsboro Point home long before the American Revolution battles would take place. History was made here right on these shores for control of these waters. So many of these stories were told over and over by Dad. History was one of the things Dad loved to talk about and on this lake there was a lot of history. When we left that summer, I felt confident in my beliefs that there was something out in the world besides the earth on which we live. There by the shoreline, on our big lake where the mountains touch the shore and the loons called to me just as this spirt world did, my soul wakened. Then so did the night sky, star by star. They showed themselves as I listened to the August crickets and wondered.

We returned from that vacation to the 1968 that was now a turbulent world. On our TV, we watched in horror the tragedy of hate and violence that took the life of Bobby Kennedy and Martin Luther King Jr., along with the hate for the Vietnam War. We saw so many protests, and our cities were in flames as buildings were burning. Our world was changing, our country was changing. The change was coming from our youth who would not tolerate a war dividing our country. The TET offensive awakened this generation in ways I did not understand at the time, but still I was well aware of the horrors of war. Horrors were easy to see as they were broadcast every night right into our living room on the nightly news. Walter Cronkite stated that the United States war in Vietnam would end in a stalemate. No winners was how I saw it.

You could hear the change as the innocent music of the early 1960s doo-wop that my sister Judy listened to was replaced by my brothers' rock and roll protesting music. The boys went from short hair to long. Needless to say, Dad wasn't too happy with the changes, and for now us Warner boys would keep our hair short! The year 1968 came to a close with the election of president Richard M. Nixon. The war in Vietnam, along with the protests, would continue creating changes in our society. These changes were not just political, but were also in science and space exploration.

On December 21, 1968, the first day of winter, Apollo 8 blasted off, and I was glued to the TV, amazed that I was seeing the first space mission to leave earth's gravity, as they described in detail what they were seeing on their way. On Christmas Eve, 180,000 miles from earth, these American astronauts would take a ride around the moon. After passing the mysterious dark side of the moon, they would orbit just sixty miles from the moon's surface while the world heard the description of what these brave men were recording. The late President Kennedy's race to put the first man on the moon and return them safely back to earth was getting closer, as was 1969.

Chapter 4

1969 - The Year That Awakened America

The year 1969 took off like the rockets on the Apollo 9 and 10 missions in such a short period of time. The United States was in a race to the moon. Richard M. Nixon took office and Dad said, If he wins, you kids will be selling pencils in the street. I was more than happy to see this was not the case. Thanks for the scare, Dad!

Dad was such a supporter of Humphrey Humphrey for his views on civil rights, but all I knew was there was so much turmoil and the news on TV was still mostly about war and the protest of the war. My brothers were fast approaching the age of the draft. Herby, my oldest brother, was in college and had a problem with his leg that he had surgery on as a young kid, so he wasn't going to have to serve, but Michael and Billy would soon face the draft and difficult decisions. We were a family that had been in every military conflict since the American Revolution, but this one was different, and I could tell both Mom and Dad did not want their children going.

That March I turned ten and one of my brother's friends gave me the peace sign and said, Hey man, peace. That was an easy thing to do, give a peace sign and say peace, but that other sign they were giving and laughing about, well Dad let me know real fast that was a curse word. Little did I know at the time how versatile that word would become over the years. We lived about a mile or so from this former church that became famous in the movie *Alice's Restaurant* and now is known as the Guthrie Center. Dad would point out hippies whenever we drove by. I thought hippies meant cool dudes and would agree with him. Little did I know at the time, but years later, my children, Katie and Dan, would end up taking cooking class there. We would go there and I wandered the church made famous in the movie. Funny how that goes, you never know where you will be in time.

Right after the church was the railroad tracks, and one day there was a little lineup as a train crossing was down. It was warm out, and I heard church bells ringing. Dad, they are ringing the church bells, I said. Little did I know the story, told around these parts for years, that they rang the church bells when the owners, Ray and Alice Brock, had sex. Damn hippies, Dad would say. I was perplexed at the time and he never explained.

Music was difficult to keep up with, but my brothers had plenty of the latest 45s. We played the top hits over and over on the record player till we could almost sing the songs word for word. We played them till the scratches were so bad that the records were finally used up. They were scratched so badly, and yet I never remember scratching any of them. The Beatles and the Doors were some of my favorites, and are to this day.

My brother Mike's friend, Kenny Aronoff, was so inspired by the Beatles he took up drums and never looked back. He took those drum sticks with him everywhere, even pounding them in the back of our family car, affectionately know as the Warner Wonder Wagon, as Mike and Kenny cruised around Stockbridge. One day many years later, we would turn on our TV to see Kenny playing at the Beatles reunion on TV. We are all so proud of Kenny for what he has achieved.

He was not the only famous musician to ever visit the Warner Homestead. Louis Armstrong stayed next door and would even play and sing. Louis would even come by this house and that thrilled Dad; naturally he became one of Dad's favorite musicians. For me, having known Kenny (who has also became one of my favorite musicians), it was him and his twin Jon, the soccer players, that inspired me. They were on my brother's high school soccer team and I could not tell one from the other. Today I can, but barely! I now know how people felt looking at my brothers, who were identical twins, and guessing which one was which.

When I got to high school, there was a ceramic wall piece that Kenny and Jon had done. I was so drawn to this that at that moment I felt I needed to learn from this piece and do my own art in clay. Though I did not get to do an art course until my senior year, I did my own clay relief just like you would a painting. This all lead to me becoming an artist years later. I appreciated the inspiration and influence they gave me. I can only hope I can return their favor to humanity as much as they did for me.

While spring for most youth meant baseball, I still preferred soccer, but was slowly beginning to accept baseball. The way to get over a fear is to understand that fear. I feared catching a hard object and missing and it hitting me! I got the brilliant idea to take apart a baseball by cutting the laces and taking out the hard part, replacing it with a tennis ball. I then went to Mom's sewing basket and got out the needle and thread and sewed the laces back up. Despite a number of pokes while sewing, my determination prevailed. Now I could toss my baseball high into the air and not worry about missing the ball and having a rock-like object bounce off my head. I began to enjoy the challenge and even watched baseball on TV. The first game that stuck in my memory was the New York Mets with Tom Seaver pitching. Little did we know those Mets would go on to be the Miracle Mets and win the World Series that year.

As spring turned to summer, we would get excited that we were going back to Lake Champlain. Also, that was the year that my sister Judy was getting married at the end of September, and that meant I would get her room when she moved out. I had my decorations ready with plenty of my favorite boat pictures. My love of boats grew with every year we went to the lake. At the cabin, we had a rowboat with a 7 1/2 horsepower Evinrude that Dad bought back in the '50s, and a little rowboat. My nephew, Keith, still has that little engine. The little white rowboat had a distinctive red trim and grey oars. Oh sure, the boat leaked water, but we had a tin quart that one could easily use to bail the water. We took turns, but my brothers preferred the boat with the 7 1/2 horsepower motor and that was just fine with me. I loved to row that little boat and did it for hours every day. Years later as an artist, I would paint that boat in my painting titled *Row Boat Etoile Filante*.

That summer of '69 we turned on our ole black and white TV to watch the blastoff of Apollo 11 from Cape Canaveral, taking Neil Armstrong, Buzz Aldrin, and Michael Collins on their mission to the moon. There was great anticipation because this mission was actually going to have them land on the moon for the first time on July 20. When they talked back and forth to mission control, there was a beep as they talked. The day they were to land on the moon, no one knew what would actually happen. Neil Armstrong slowly flew the Lunar Module to the surface of the moon and made his famous quote: "That's one small step for man, one giant leap for mankind." Dad commented how Grandpa would have loved seeing this day, as he was such a supporter of president John Kennedy, who wanted the United States to be the first on the moon. The moment felt a little patriotic and scientific at the same time. My only thought was that I hoped they could return back to earth, as the splashdowns into the ocean to return were dangerous, too. Now that the

Apollo 11 mission was done, my thoughts turned to going back up to Lake Champlain.

I made an extra Tommy baseball to take up with me and by now was getting better at catching the ball. Soccer always came so easily to me, but not baseball. Everyone in the neighborhood could play baseball. The Baer family down the lane from us had three boys and they all could play with ease, though Max was by far the best of the three, and the most kind to me. Still, not fitting in was getting old for me, and I was determined to get better at this all-American pastime. Oh sure, I played most other games like Outs in basketball on our homemade basketball hoop, but baseball was the game most played back then. Bit by bit, I was starting to really like the game of catch, but I was terrible at hitting. Forget all that, because now my thoughts now turned to going back to my Lake Champlain.

The night before, Dad would pack up the ole '68 blue Warner Wonder Wagon. That summer we all helped and were so excited to go. Early rise was the word of the day. Mom and Dad had us on the road by 5:15 AM. I used think they did that so we would sleep and Dad would have peace driving, but the truth was he could hardly wait to get there himself. We would take Route 22 north all the way to Willsboro.

At the lake, my thoughts turned to swimming and the little rowboat. The cabin also had a great out-of-tune piano that we took turns playing on rainy days, but every sunny day we were outside as much as possible. I would take the little rowboat down the lake about four cabins below ours. Here I started to meet kids that would come back year after year, some I am still close with. There are so many great memories, but the biggest impact was spent at night on our sandy beach with campfires. I looked forward to Dad telling stories, having s'mores, and singing. Mom loved when we sang as it gave her a feeling of closeness between her boys. We sang songs Mom liked that had that religious feel to them. "Found a Peanut," for example was about a kid who ate a peanut, died, and went to heaven only to find out he was dreaming. "All Night, All

Day," was another one of Mom's favorite from us kids, but she loved when Dad would sing "Shine On Harvest Moon" or "Moon Light In Vermont," and her favorite, "Show Me the Way to Go Home."

I remember one particular campfire that would forever change my life. Mom had just gone up to the cabin and my older brothers were off somewhere. At that moment, I looked at the gleaming reflective lights of Burlington and got a gut feeling, just like I did when I was much younger in Port Henry. Dad looked towards Vermont and turned to tell a story, only I was seeing fear in his eyes and oh boy, at that point he had my attention. Dad pointed across the lake while telling the story. His boss and his wife were staying over in Vermont, out in the country, and while his wife was out walking, he stayed home reading. She came home in a panic, saying a UFO was out in the field. The husband told his wife they could go out and look tomorrow. So the next day, they went out for a walk where she said she saw the object. Sure enough, there was a perfect circle of burnt grass about forty feet wide. See, I told you, do you believe me now? she said.

I could see the fear in Dad's eyes as he said, Kids, if you ever see one of these UFOs just run! I found it strange that Dad would tell this story and felt there was more to the story than Dad was willing to tell. Dad didn't give a warning that often, so when he did I listened. That night as I went to sleep with those lapping waves, I began to wonder about those feelings of messages I was hearing in my mind; soon I would find out what they were, when we returned to the Berkshires and Great Barrington and the now famous 1969 Labor Day.

Chapter 5

A UFO Comes to the Berkshires

I remember Labor Day weekend 1969 like it was yesterday. The weather was rather hot, nearing ninety degrees with calm winds. My thoughts of more time down in our cool brook were a big part part of my plans that weekend. The brook was always rather cold and refreshing in our youth, but downright freezing to adults. The brook that flowed out of the Berkshire Mountain range was cold enough to chill a penguin. This was the last weekend before we had to go back to school, so I wanted to do as much as possible. I dreaded the back-to-school order that was about to go into effect, and to say I was not a fan of going to school was an understatement. Dad would remind us that, If your Mother and I have to go to work, then you kids have to go to school. Sorry, kids, summer vacation is over!

Before I knew it, Sunday morning rolled in, and going to 7 AM mass would give me more time to do fun things. On the way back from church, Mom let me know she wanted me to go with her and Dad to see my Nana, who now was living out her life with my Aunt Linnie and her children. Mom was very insistent that I should go with her and Dad, and so I did. After a good breakfast, we headed out for the day. I wasn't happy to go, but could tell they were happy I was there.

My aunt and cousins lived in a three-story old brownstone in the village of Lansingburgh in North Troy, New York. This was the house that Mom grew up in, and she would tell us stories of what it was like in her day. What I liked about their location most was they had a great deli store nearby, along with a Schwinn bicycle store. I would just about drool looking at those bikes, some of the best made at the time. Oh, and that deli, my, oh my, what a great sandwich shop!

Aunt Linnie always made piles of great sandwiches and had bags of potato chips and ice-cold Coca-Cola. Her blind dog would always beg for food and always managed to get us to give in and donate some scraps under the table, which he graciously accepted. That was a trade-off for not growling at me; besides there were always seconds at the Gherighty household. This trip, however, everyone was very gloomy and serious.

Nana was dying from cancer, something I didn't understand at ten years old. Mom reminded me I still had Monday left, and that Nana would love to see me. I was more than happy to go to visit Nana, but little did I know it would be the last time I saw her alive. You have to hold fast to your loved ones, and on that day I did, sitting a long time on the couch with Nana, just holding her hand. While on the couch, Dad took my picture with Nana, one I will forever cherish. Later that day, on the way home hardly a word was spoken; I could feel Mother's pain just in her silence. Mom would make sure Monday would be a cheerier day.

Monday, September 1, 1969, started out like any typical Labor Day here in the Berkshires. Although summer time was winding down in our town, out here in Seekonk, the summer felt like it would be endless. The weather called for very hot temperatures which meant brook time would be perfect. Right after a quick lunch and of course, Mom's thirty-minute wait time for our lunch to digest, we all headed down for the day. We were in the water and out of the water till we shivered and Dad finally said, OK kids, that's enough. When Dad said enough, then we stopped and reluctantly got out of the mountain brook.

This was one of the last times to swim for the summer. Soon Dad and my older brothers would take out the center of the Warner swimming pool dam which was made of rocks, and then reinforce our second dam, where our water well was. This was a right of passage from summer to fall at the Warner Homestead.

Getting your water from a brook to a pump house and then having the water pumped all the way up to our house on the hill was rather difficult. September would end the summer fun, and soon work would be underway for the fall preparation that all us boys would chip in and help with. Preparation for winter's certainty was a natural, timely matter and we would find ways to make theses chores fun. That was Dad's way of teaching us not to complain about work and to enjoy whatever we were doing.

Suppertime came, and Mom made a light supper. After that I asked to go next door to the Shaw's to do coloring with Debbie. When I got there, we watched TV for a while and played some board games before coloring. We had the record player going and I would do a funny dance to "Wipe Out" by The Surgaris, and of course this made Debbie laugh. We went back to coloring, as I knew I could only stay till just after sunset. I was in my zone with those Crayola crayons, concentrating and staying in the lines. Debbie gave her approval of my fine work within the lines and choice of colors.

This determination of concentrating was a lesson that would serve me well later in life as an artist. So there we were, just coloring in our books and listening to 45s on the record player when I heard something so powerful that I instantly got chills and the hairs on my arms went straight up. My heart began to beat faster and faster as I stood up. I realized it was in my mind, just like at Lake Champlain the first time at Willsboro Point when I looked to the northeast towards Burlington and sensed something was communicating to me. As I walked over to the window to have a look, Debbie asked, Aren't we still coloring? Slowly I answered, No, I don't think so. My life was about to turn to the unexplainable and in a moment's notice would forever change how I looked at the universe. Although I had many times felt mental telepathy, this experience would be conclusive to me that it was real and the feeling was overwhelming. The feeling was hard to explain and was not a thought, but a demand.

I looked towards the east and towards the lights of Simon's Rock College. The communication told me they were at Lake Mansfield, just over the hill from the college. The Rock was an early college, meaning you could go there for your last two years of high school. We lived just a half mile from the college. I didn't know who they were, but the message was simple, clear, and precise, and that was for me to go home right away.

I looked to Debbie and said, I have to go home right away, I think God is talking to me from those clouds. Being raised Catholic, who or what could possibly send me a message like that? I felt an awful and frantic panic set in to run home as fast as I could.

With the adrenaline that now filled my ten-year-old body, I started to rush for the door. I only got the words, I have to go home, out to Gram. I caught the look of Jane, Debbie's sister, and the fright on her face made me even more scared. Running out of the Shaw house, fear filled me by the millisecond. Now I was a fast kid, a really fast kid. I wasn't good at baseball, but I could outrun almost any most kid I knew. On this night, I thought I could outrun a deer.

After opening their door, you went though one room to a coal room which had no light on, and added to my adrenaline flow. From the coal room, it was a short ten feet to the outdoors. Once outside, I ran as fast as my feet would take me across their driveway. Just as I got to the big rock, the first rock on the path from the Shaw house to the Warner Homestead, I felt the presence of something I had never felt. As I turned to my left, my eyes opened wide to a surreal site just thirty-five feet above me.

At that moment, all the noise of nature was stripped away in complete silence. Even the noisy September crickets and all other noise was gone in an instant. Nothing, no noise at all. There before me, a UFO had dropped out of the sky, just after the golden hour of sunset had passed. Everything went into slow motion, as if I was walking slowly, but wasn't moving at all.

The surreal scene in front of me was overwhelming to take in; a UFO was just thirty-five feet above me, floating in place. The craft was so close I could see the lights going in one direction, a second part of the craft going the other. My eyes were fixated on this object in amazement and fear at the same time. The lights on the UFO were colors I had never seen before. I can't explain it other than to say that they were just different than earth colors.

The UFO was about forty feet wide and maybe twenty-five feet tall. The top section glowed, and the first set of lights that went around the ship were surreal. I was so taken aback by the colors. The main part of the ship was a silver metallic with a slight green tinge to that color. A second set of lights were just under the top set and the bottom section seemed to be going in an opposite direction as the craft just hovered without making any noise. I was stunned, taking in this world changing event and the lack of sounds around me. How could the noise be gone? Even the September crickets just disappeared. In that instant, from the bottom of that UFO, a beam came on me. My arms jerked back, taking my gasping deep breath away, as if when you come up from water.

My memories on the craft were that of fear and taking in images, the first being seeing a girl crouched down to my right. The look of fear in her eyes was haunting and her expression, pleading for help, was so frightening. Just seeing the fear in her eyes was overwhelming. I was aware of other children, but would look down to avoid seeing them. I saw other species of beings, both human-like and others, but the overwhelming memory was the silence and lights. I remember seeing a table and instruments on a panel. Then the whole episode was over rather quickly.

I blinked my eyes and in that warped time of seven minutes, I was put back down at the other end of the Shaw property, fifteen or more feet off the path. I was laid down flat on my back now facing the Shaw house with the UFO beam on me. I was set down the same gentle way you would place an infant into a crib. Then one of my brothers was calling to me, and I heard Bo's voice scream, RUN TOMMY! I yelled back, I can't! It's holding me down.

I was stunned that this bright beam of light could literally hold me in place. Over and over I kept thinking, How could this be? As scared as I was, none of my brothers were coming to my rescue. Actually, I didn't blame them and if they were scared, you can imagine how I felt.

Now, not moving, the beings used mental telepathy to speak to me, letting me know I was OK and they would be done in a minute. At that moment I stopped struggling and let my body relax; after all, they were in control. The minute passed and sure enough, they let me know they were done. What their purpose was with me has been the long-lasting life question. As soon as they let me know the event was now over, the beam which took me away, returned me, and then held me in place on the ground was turned off. This beam, the brightest white and blue haze you could imagine, was turned off and I was free and allowed to stand up. What the hell? I thought. This is crazy and it's so close.

Now just staring up at the UFO, my thought was: If I had a baseball in my hand, I could probably hit that craft just above me. Probably would not have been a good idea anyways. Maybe that was me just trying to take some control back in my mind; at this point, I had absolutely none.

The UFO slowly began to rise to clear the trees in our yard and then went slowly towards the west, down towards Division Street. I took one look at Bo huddled against the garage door. I was trying to take in what had just happened. The entire event was so surreal that comprehending the situation went past fright and amazement to a flight reaction.

I was stunned, to say the least, and with my feet not failing me now, I bolted into our house. Passing the telephone in our hall was the last thing

I remembered that night. I had not even a drop of a recollection after that until the next morning; I was for sure still in a state of shock.

Even the next morning when I woke, I was still so shaken up. No one said anything about what had happened the night before. Bo just looked at me, shaking his head. I remember eating a breakfast of frosted flakes then going to iron my school pants, but realizing we still had one more day till school opened. My mom questioned why I was ironing my first-day-of-school pants. Just getting stuff ready ahead of time, came my answer.

Like every morning in the Warner Homestead, our radio was turned on to 860 on the AM dial to WSBS and the seven o'clock newscast. Tom J did the morning news, and he started off by saying, Something funny was going on in the South Berkshires, as people were reporting seeing a UFO over the South Berkshires. Perhaps it wasn't swamp gas after all. I didn't know what swamp gas was but I was sure glad I wasn't the only one to see this craft. I wondered who else may have seen it and if they had the same thing happen to them the way I did.

Tom J and the WSBS statement was simple, nothing more than that statement. Some went on to say he said a lot of details that day, but that was plain hogwash. However, twenty years later, in 1989, there was a program on WSBS on the subject of UFOs, but not necessarily the one from 1969. The 1989 program had many people calling in, and I did as well, but too late to go on the air. Whoever I spoke with knew who I was.

You must be one of the Warner Boys from Seekonk, they said. We saw the UFO over your house that night! I just didn't even bother to take note of who the woman was, but was happy to have a confirmation of what happened. It took years for people to come forward and talk in public about the subject of the night of September 1, but on September 2, 1969, very few were willing to talk.

Today, over fifty years later, many people have come forward and I suspect many more may yet. I talked about that night to close friends, but for the most part no one wanted to open up, and I didn't blame them.

Apparently, the subject was very taboo. Perhaps they felt scared or vulnerable that not talking would make the whole event go away. For me, however, the event was only the beginning.

I was told that the next day my Mom went over and talked to Gram about what happened, but not ever a word was said to me. I was at the Shaw's the next day and Jane said to me, Tommy, you were out of it, barely speaking. I must have just turned to my crayons and coloring book for peace. Although many knew what happened, no one really wanted to talk. When I went back to school, hardly a word was spoken about the subject, and that was just fine with me because I didn't know how to explain what I saw and experienced that fateful night.

Dad warned us earlier about these UFOs and I never said a word to him about it nor did he say anything to me until near the end of his life. He tried to explain to me that he had seen a UFO as well. The silence was my mother's influence: if you didn't talk about something, then perhaps it would go away, like it never happened. That was the theory, that life would go on if you did. You would forget the event; but for me, this was just not the case. I had changed and would have more and more questions than answers after being abducted. I would remember the UFO, so surreal, floating in place there in the field between our two houses. In time, more and more events would happen and I would feel even more isolated because of my events, bringing an empty, yet reflecting feeling to my soul.

Years later, just before Gram died, she asked her granddaughter Jane, Did anyone figure out what happened to Tommy that night? Is Tommy OK today? Jane knew what she was asking. No Gram, and yes he's OK now. I was one of the last thoughts Gram talked about, as she died the very next day.

I remember when I asked Jane what she had seen, and hearing Jane talk, I felt like I was back to that frightful night. Her word just stuck with me. She said, Gram yelled to me, What is Tommy doing? as Jane asked the same thing back to Gram. He is running in that light and not moving, was her response. She continued telling the part of the story I had not heard her confirm. Tommy, in a flash you disappeared in the beam and were gone. You were gone for about seven minutes and ended up returned in that beam again at the other end of the property by your garden. I thought about that for years, knowing there were not many who have witnessed a UFO beam or have disappeared in that beam.

My details of that night that I was abducted by a UFO may be limited, but the things I did remember remain clear to this day. There were others there, and in time I would find out who that girl crouched to my right was when I entered hight school at Monument Mountain. I opened a door just as she was coming through and the hairs on my arm stood straight up in fright. I followed her to her class and asked some people who she was. I just had to know. Yet even knowing, I still said noting to her. The pain and fear in her eyes was both overwhelming and haunting. We reconnected not long ago and today, over fifty years later, that girl, Melanie, and her husband, Henry, are very close friends of ours. We opened up telling our stories of that surreal and frightful night. I have memories, but kept some of those memories to myself out of fear of ridicule.

The event on September 1, 1969, was not just about one person as was promoted both through the media and UFO conferences. There was even a monument erected to one person, stating his was the first off-world incident. He had experiences similar to mine. But he wasn't the first that night nor was he the last.

The part that frustrates me the most was the silence that prevailed. How could a UFO come within thirty-five feet and no one want to talk about what had happened? This emptied my soul and made me feel so alone that no one would talk to me. When I did bring up the subject, whoever I was talking to just changed the subject in a hurry.

Jane continued, The next day, Gram talked to your Mom about what had happened. You never said anything the next day and were quiet as a mouse. I was quiet because I must have still been in shock! Not only did Jane not say anything to me, nor did Gram, nor did my own mom or dad. Oh, Mom's Irish ways of if you didn't talk about what had happened, then in time you would forget about the event. Ah, but now over fifty years later we still talk about that unforgettable and frightful historic September 1, 1969, night.

Chapter 6

Two Weeks Later And Back Again

School was going as well as school could go. I would have rather it stayed like a Beach Boys summer song, but that wasn't going to happen. Even the Great Barrington Fair was now over, which was another sign the last of summer was behind us and soon fall would be here. Going from summer to fall and the routine of just being in school never gave me the warm fuzzies. I kept thinking someone would ask about the UFO and I wasn't one to take teasing lightly. I would gladly talk about what happened, but teasing was not acceptable. The weather was still warm, and on the weekends actually very pleasant, and I wanted to hang on to that summer spirit just a little longer.

My days were spent with a few more swims in the now very chilly Alford Book and by having a catch by myself, practicing by throwing my soft baseball in the air and catching it again. By now I was even joining in the neighborhood baseball games. I still wasn't very good, but at least I felt like I somewhat fit in, and that was important to me. Two weeks after that Labor Day, I was happy and surprised when my brother asked if I wanted to have a catch. I wasn't too keen, being we were getting closer to sunset, but there was enough time. I had been keeping to myself and perhaps he was trying to get me to open up after what had happened just two weeks prior. No matter the reason, I cherished any brother time when there was no competition. Just a catch, Tommy, he said.

I wasn't sure where his twin was at the time, but I recall him wanting to watch TV. I just wanted to have a catch and there was enough sunlight to toss it for a while. We went out to what we called the tennis court. Years ago it was a pristinely maintained clay court for guests at our Warner Homestead bed and breakfast, one of the first in the Berkshires. Now in 1969, the tennis court was covered in grass and was a perfect flat place to play games and a natural place to have a catch. The sun had just set and the colors were very vivid, as I recall of this event. The event was fast, but in reality was not fast at all. My understanding of time over the years is that time is rather complex subject, especially time that is lost, and in this case, there was a considerable amount of lost time.

I threw the ball to my brother and he tossed it to me. Back and forth about four times, and then in a second, another wild event happened. Back and forth we tossed the ball, then I threw the ball and it went about fifteen feet, then changed directions and went past me! How can that be? I thought, as I now was drowning in a foggy sate of confusion, chasing down the ball. Then a second thought hit me: Oh my God, it was now dark. In an instant, we had lost a considerable amount of time, nearly forty-five minutes. Right away I thought, How can that be? And over and over in my mind I repeated that question to myself. I threw the ball and the ball reversed direction and just went right past me.

I was frantic to take this all in while chasing down the ball, now headed for the road. Just as I picked up the ball, two more of my brothers, Mike and Billy (Rosco), and Jane's brother were running up from the brook, and he was yelling, Did you see the UFO? It was right over Tommy's head. Look, it's right up there! Sure enough, up in the sky you could see the UFO hovering in one spot, off in the distance, not moving at all, just staying in one spot. I felt a presence telepathically communicating to me even from that distance, just like it had done two weeks prior as I was held under that bright beam. No doubt they came back for me again, and the mystery of why would be a life-long question.

In a split second, the UFO went across the sky, stopped a second time, and held that position for a minute before departing. In a blink of an eye it was gone, vanished faster than a lightning bolt strike on a dark summer night. A vivid image taken in and then gone, leaving behind the vast night sky, and no explanation to their destination, and us boys dumbfounded.

Instantly, my mind raced to try and unravel the moments. Wait, I thought the stars were out? I took in what was in front of me and I realized the truth: that I had lost a considerable amount of time, but wasn't about to say anything to my brothers. From the time of the sun going down to those first stars appearing takes at least forty-five minutes. Oh, I remembered running back into our homestead farmhouse like I was propelled by a Saturn Five rocket. Why me? I kept thinking as I bolted into the house, feeling like these UFOs wanted something from me, but what, I just couldn't comprehend. I had no detailed memory of what took place other than foggy images. I must have gone into a state of shock for the second time in two weeks. No doubt I was abducted again, and my fear of the unknown had to be conquered. To have a UFO so close twice in two weeks was more than I could take.

Oh heck, now I was afraid to go out at night for quite some time. The only distraction I had now was my sister getting married soon, and I would get her bedroom. After all this drama, I would be happy to have the comfort of knowing my parents were in the next room. It was much needed reassurance for this ten-year-old. I figured sleeping would be easy in my new room, but oh, no. Slumber eluded me and I was wakened often by flashbacks, taking me onto the UFO. It was so much for me to take in, images of being on a UFO, seeing things I had no idea what they were, and telepathic messages I tried to ignore but eventually listened to. My mind was now flooded with questions to which no one would have answers to and no one was really willing to talk about.

After these close encounters, I would have vivid dreams of a far away planet and also images of being on the UFO. Now, if you stop and think of your life, you can have images recalled and brought back up to see them in your mind. This is like a homemade movie, but how did they get in there, in your mind? As humans, this is done by living and recalling the event. We observe an event using our senses and then that event is absorbed by the thalamus and frontal lobe of our brains. The more dramatic our event, the more neurons are fired to make the event even clearer, and thus easier to recall, even those we do not particularly want to store. Mine must have been firing like the finale of a Fourth of July fireworks show. Our stored information does not have a delete button; that is not an option. No matter the encoding type for humans, from acoustic to visual, tactile, or semantic, we are like computers, taking information then storing that information for a later recall.

I began to wonder over the years about how this movie-like memory of a distant planet and life got deep in to my recording device as a human. My conclusion was that, however the memory got there, only a far greater intelligence could pull that off. I went from feeling like I was cursed to feeling that I was blessed for having insight very few have. I suppose that would make me a visionary, but for me the two lives blended both talents and ideas. For example, as an artist I can paint both consciously and subconsciously. While just thinking of a subject, they appear in the painting without me actually being aware I was putting that in a background.

My book cover is a good example. For instance, if your eyes relax, you will see an alien reaching down for me, and below the UFO you will see the number 69. At the time I was doing the painting, I was thinking of the year and of course painting the UFO beam on me, I was thinking about aliens. However the most important gift was put deep within my soul and is what makes my human character cry out. The gift is understanding and feeling tied to the true meaning of unconditional love. Perhaps this is why I am an artist and poet, trying to express what is within my soul, things once lived far, far away and replicated here on earth.

So what if your life movie was put in you, only you didn't live that life? Or did you? What is considered having lived a life? Is it pictures? And if not pictures, are they memories? Complex thoughts of parallel universes and past lives? I kept much of this to myself and besides, who the hell would believe me? Well, maybe some did at that time. If all this wasn't bad enough, from time to time I would have orbs that would appear in my room.

These orbs floating in were like balls of psychic energy that just appeared in my room, but where did they come from and were they there to help me or hurt me? I never said a word about the orbs till years later, but they scared the daylights out of me. Despite my fear, I took in the mystic nature of telepathic messages and energy with an inquisitive nature that any ten-year-old abductee would have, seeking answers at every corner of my life.

One night before sleeping in my new room, orbs had appeared and I insisted my older brothers check the roof, as I was so sure after seeing an orb that surely a UFO must be right over our house. My brothers made me look to see this was not the case, and though I was relieved there was no UFO, the energy orbs still had me scared. My brother Michael reassured me a number of times there were none there, and so back into the homestead we went. Taking to myself, I said, I need to sleep and if anyone finds out I slept with a teddy bear, that would be tease central at school, so I kept that to myself.

So along with my teddy, I had to find a way to sleep; and I learned how and as it turned out, what I was doing was visualization. Self-taught visualization long before the word was even used by psychologists. My lessons were taught by mental telepathy from a far-off source. How could I find a distraction? And the idea came to me. My older brother Michael had gotten some glow goo and wrote on his walls, cause this was cool. *Cool* was in back in 1969. He wrote Schlitz on his wall and wrote his girlfriend's name on his 1969 Rheingold Extra Dry beer sign. There may have even been a peace sign painted for the times as well. So I got what was left of that goo and went to work.

There was a girl in my class named Joanne Thompson and she was really funny. While so many seemed serious, Joanne made me smile and laugh, even though my laugh was concealed to myself. I didn't reveal this to Joanne till years and years later. To this day, she reassures me we are forever friends. Turns out she even did stand up comedy, so my assessment of my classmate was right! Joanne (JT) just made everyone smile with her bubbly personality. So I put our initials on the ceiling with the glowing goo and before I went to sleep, I would stare at the ceiling thinking of my funny and kind classmate. With my teddy bear in my arms and laughs on my face, I went to sleep. Distraction and visualization was the only way I could get to sleep. To this day, I still can't just fall asleep at night. Slumber had its moments, but since writing this book, I have to work at sleeping even more.

I didn't tell JT about this until a few years back. Turns out JT had a close encounter of her own; not only had JT had an encounter, but her distant cousins also had an encounter the same night as me on September 1, 1969. Theirs was at Lake Mansfield in Great Barrington, right where I was told the UFO was as I looked out from the Shaw's that fateful night. That fall, we also heard that two students saw the UFO over Simon's Rock just before it came over the Shaw's property and Warner Homestead. I never got to know who they were, but hearing that they fainted in shock was eyeopening to me.

I wanted to hide that this all happened to me for fear of being teased, but it was far more than that. I began to wonder if somehow they knew where I was, because no doubt this UFO had me leave the Shaw's by mental telepathy. Blocking this out was impossible, but I did learn to deal with sleeping through visualization. Just how long could a ten-year-old hide that he slept with his teddy bear? I hid this from my brothers, and years later as young adult, I put that teddy in my first pick up truck. For years, Teddy sat on the dash of my 77' Ford F-100 I named Tuck. Some people name a boat and I named my truck. Along with Teddy was a special gift of inspiration, a small soccer ball that hung from the mirror. Tuck is long gone, but made it through half of the states. Teddy remains with me to this day, having traveled much of the eastern United States to Canada, and back to the Warner Homestead.

I became very quiet after the second abduction and stayed home a lot, not wanting to visit next door for fear of what might happen next. There was something else I now had, an instinct like a protective shield, that there were good forces and bad. After the second UFO event, I spent much of my time alone. I learned that I loved art and I loved soccer because both could be perfected by myself. However, at this point I still was not a good baseball player. My bravery would have to protect my deep secrets of having had such close encounters. So forward I would go, because back then you keep this stuff to yourself. Like I said, a number of times I thought, Besides who would believe me anyway? It turned out there were more of us than I thought possible.

One day, a number of years after the abductions, I was at catechism (Catholic religion school for those who may not know), where I had an incident that changed how I felt about my church. Not about my spiritual beliefs, but the views of the Catholic church that I faithfully attended since birth. I felt that there must be something to all this universe stuff and was in a conversation with a few of my classmates. Somehow, someone picked up what we were talking about and said to one of our priests that I had seen a UFO. He looked at me, putting his arm around me and said, You must have Satan in you. As he glared into my eyes, I felt anger and sadness all at the same time. As if his arm around me was going to reassure me that he was going to take out Satan, and with what? What was I to do next, an act of contrition? I had no such sins to confess because this was not Satan in me, but my recall of a traumatic event. I was bullshit angry as I abruptly pulled away and walked right out the door. I walked the nearly three miles home, all the way fuming and thinking, How dare he say such a thing. I questioned if I even belonged in this church. I never told anyone what he had said, as I was too hurt. I was thirteen now, and would no longer question myself about my encounters with a UFO, because deep down I knew he was a nonbeliever and I was the one who was right. He was limited in his thinking and I refused to even entertain a conversation about what was good and what was evil. In my mind I was ready to throw f-bombs at that priest, but my Mom always said if you don't have anything good to say, then don't say it. Despite my anger, I held my thoughts close to the vest because my fear of ridicule was overwhelming to me, and I kept those f-bombs tucked in my proverbial pocket.

The year I had turned thirteen, we went to Lake Champlain and I had the first of many bizarre meetings with people who came in contact with UFOs. I had just taken a swim out to the Buena Vista Park raft and had a few jumps into the refreshing water. I remember there were a few kids out on the dock. They called, See you later. I have to head home. With that, I dove off the dock into the deep water and swam back to the shore, feeling once again self-confident and good about myself. At first, I didn't notice this kid swimming in at the same time, as he was behind me until we got to the shallow water where we could stand.

I wasn't the best swimmer, but a good dive in and a little swimming and you were back on the beach. This kid was about my age and he approached me. He said hello, then went right into the UFO talk. You know about UFOs, he said to me. I had never met the kid and we were not talking about the subject on the dock, so at this point I didn't want to talk about my experiences. I denied I had. Back and forth this went a bit, until I asked how he would know that. Then without hesitation, he stunned me with his answer: Because I was on that UFO and I remember you. I nearly fell over at his response. I don't even recall my response, but I no longer wanted to talk about the subject.

For many years, I would know him but avoided talking about that subject. To think someone remembered me on that UFO... He was the first but not the last to say such a thing to me about UFO abductions.

A few years ago I just nicknamed him X, because he no longer wanted to talk on the subject. Sure, now I wanted to talk about the subject and no matter how much I tried to have him open up, X went silent. Just because I was opening up about the subject doesn't mean the next person would want to. You have to respect their choice and if they do not want to talk, then that is fine. The main reason for my coming forward was to help others do the same if they chose to. Not for X though, he was burnt toast and done, so I let it go forever with X, and in my mind wish him peace and happiness.

So much for this going away. Still, I felt peace at the lake and I began to once again enjoy the night sky, the magic of the stars above, the love of looking at the moon reflecting on the water. Nature, you see, is not to be feared, I thought, but cherished and appreciated, just like what was out in the universe. Now I feared not the night sky nor anything else out in nature, however the ridicule of the events began to silence me. My inner circle of those I would talk to would shrink to a minimum of my very close friends. I kept my thoughts safe, for if you would get ridiculed from your priest and have him say you had Satan in you, then who else could a now young teen trust?

Despite all this, life went on and when we left Lake Champlain for Great Barrington, my mind was consumed with just trying to fit in. Some new kids moved in just up the road to the property that at one time belonged to my great-aunt and -uncle. The family had three boys and one girl. The girl, Annah, was the oldest and was my age, and her brother, Jake, was next closest to me in age. They were a very athletic family and also very intelligent. Annah and I would eventually graduate from Monument Mountain High School together, but in high school we ran in different social groups and didn't get to spend hardly any time together, as we did when we were younger.

Her father was into baseball and the Cincinnati Reds. I remember when I met him the first time, he sat me down on a Saturday to watch some baseball. With the distinct aroma of his pipe filling the air, he announced, The Big Red Machine is on. The what? I thought and my expression gave away my ignorance of the subject. He said, You know, Pete Rose, Johnny Bench... Oh, sit down, Tommy, and watch. That was the day I was hooked on watching baseball, right there at their home. I am still thankful to this day that I took his advice.

The twins and I would go up to their house often to play baseball and different games. With them having an old barn, we would play hide-and-seek that would last for hours. Don't ask me why, but one day we took our bikes up on the barn roof on a dare, and from then on, more dares would follow. I was more than willing to do crazy acts just to try and fit in with the other kids. No one was topping my bravery—or in my case, downright stupidity. They dared me to ride off the barn roof. Not that I really wanted to, but I had no choice. They dared me in front of Annah, who had all the neighborhood boys' fancy, and of course her cousins, who just loved to tease me to no end. Eventually, their teasing would send me away, never to return. That was as bad as the triple-dog dare and so I was game on.

So on my bike with a sissy bar and my triple-dog dare, I headed off the roof. I just knew it was a mistake after the first few feet, but there was no turning back and as I went off the roof, I instantly experienced the separation of time. My fall all went in slow motion, giving me the time to react. I let go of the bike and as I hit the ground, went into a roll then bounced up to catch the bike at the same time. I jumped back on the bike all in one motion and rode around to the front of the barn where they all could see the conquering hero. I was thrilled and shocked at my Irish luck, but still perplexed how time went into slow motion. I instantly thought back to 1969 and my encounters; how they, too, were affected by time. Just how did I do that?

Oh sure, I was the one who would take on the proverbial triple-dog dare to ride off a barn roof like Evel Knievel, but only because of my want to fit in after the UFO talk that had gone around. I was so self-conscious at that age. Of course, I knew at the start when down the roof I went that it was dangerous and a bad idea. The smart side of me said, Oh, no, don't do it, but was overruled by my stupidity and desire to fit in; and I do mean stupidity! Riding my bike back around in victory, I knew it looked as if I rode right off that barn roof, but no way was going to let them all know the truth, as they were now up on the roof and I was safely on the ground. Around the corner, Mrs. T had just came out the farmhouse door, and looking up at them all on the roof yelled, You kids get off that roof right now. At least Tommy has some common sense. I even thought I heard Jake laugh and say, Yeah, right.

Later that summer, in September of 1971, that crazy daredevil Evel Knievel actually came to the Great Barrington Fair. I still have the autograph he gave me somewhere signed, "To Tommy, Happy Landings, Evel Knievel." I think half the town was at the fair that night as he made his jump over sixteen cars, then crashed to the ground just before a pile of hay bales at the end of his runway. Some kids at the last minute jumped up on the bales to have a great look. My brothers Michael and Rosco (Billy) were two of those teens. Knievel was supposed to make an even larger jump, but it was postponed because he was banged up pretty bad and was so mad at security for letting those kids on the bales of hay. It was Knievel's destiny not to perform a second jump, and he left Great Barrington the next day. I had some of that daredevil in me, and perhaps pushing the envelope to prove my self and trying to fit in wasn't such a good idea, but it was often a factor in dangerous behavior.

On another close call after a heavy rain, my brother John and I went for a swim. That's too high to go in, John, I said. John just looked at me. Oh come on, Tommy, that's nothing. You got this, you go first. I wanted my brothers to see me as brave and fearless. They were never ones to back down, and if they weren't, then neither was I. I suppose being the youngest in a pack of tough boys was influential, too. The second I went in, I knew this was a very, very bad idea, actually downright stupid. Here we go again, I thought, as time went into slow motion as if to confirm I was in trouble. I was aiming just to get to the other side and was going down the swollen brook faster than Mark Spitz in an olympic swimming final. I made it to the other side just before our dam and the wicked rapids. John, with his humor to break up my anger, joked with me and asked if I was going to swim back, but I must have had a look, and he said, OK, I'll bring your sneakers home, see you when you get back. In bare feet and a pair of shorts, I tromped thought the tall grass and brambles to make it to the nearby Alford Road, then walked around the block home.

My bare feet hurt so badly, but even worse than that, they smelled horrible. You see, I had to walk past the Shaw Farm at the bottom of our Seekonk hill and could not avoid the cow manure that was all over our road. Sometimes, I thought Nat, their farmhand, did that on purpose to quicken his chores of getting rid of the daily manure! At this point, I was sore and mad as hornet at John. With my feet now covered in cow manure, I was really steaming, and of course, John was laughing. I got home and got the hose out to wash my feet and John made the standard request: Let's not tell Ma. Us Warner boys would take years to get proper common sense. We were tough kids then and so happy Ma never knew half of all the stupid things we did. Along with rough play, we had rough work to do, and not only at home. Dad made sure we went out and learned how to work for others and make a dollar. Work ethics were taught to us young in our household, and we learned how to handle them properly. At thirteen years old, I already had a few lawn care jobs, but I never forgot my first account.

Chapter 7

The Judge, The Mob, and Me

Oh yes, my first job and account turned out to more than a first job. Now at thirteen years old, this job was a healing and growing process. I was very quiet after my close encounters and I think Dad must have thought doing work would be a help. At the bottom of our hill lived an interesting family; most in our neighborhood were interesting in some way, but this topped them all. That Sunday, we had just gone to church then stopped for doughnuts at the Spudnut Shop before picking up the Sunday paper. Dad picked up theirs as well, and we planed to drop off the paper before heading home for Sunday breakfast. Back then, we were told no breakfast before church. I'm sure that was so we could all be on time. Mom, who worked nights, would be ready to go just a few minutes before 7 AM and Dad would drop us off to park the car to make it on time. The mass had more like 7:05 start time, and I often thought Ma had something to do with that.

The doughnuts were the reward for me, and after mass we were ready to order. You had to get doughnuts early because they sold fast on Sunday. You also wanted to go early before many people got to sit down and smoke with their coffee and sweets. You were allowed to smoke in restaurants back then, so if you got your doughnuts before the smokers, your doughnuts wouldn't have that slight taste and aroma of cigarettes. So with doughnuts and papers we headed to the neighbor's house to drop off their paper. Dad went in and when he came back out, he proudly announced the good news: Tommy, you now have your first job and will be mowing the Keogh's lawn. My brothers grinned, one saying, Great, Tommy! Why are they grinning? They must have known something I didn't.

I don't know why I had to be the last to know why most of the kids in the neighborhood were afraid of the Keoghs and would not work there, but to heck with them, I had my first job. I was to get twelve dollars for mowing their lawn and they provide the gas and mower that was self-propelled. How easy is that, a self-propelled mower! That was nothing compared to using our push-by-hand mower up the side of the hill. I started the next Saturday and was a bit nervous, but Mrs. Keogh calmed me down as soon as she explained how the self-propelled mower worked, and I was off and going. Though the mower was a bit slow, the ease of operation was quite pleasant, as was my thought of earning cash.

The Keoghs were Irish Catholic and Mom and Dad loved them. After mowing the lawn, Mrs. Keogh would make lunch for me and Mr. Keogh. She always made me a bologna sandwich cut into two triangles with chips, a pickle, and an ice-cold Coca-Cola. She would say, You boys, your lunch is ready, and we would sit out on their screened in porch off their kitchen or out at the table in the yard with a nice umbrella. There was something special about this place and at first I could not understand. I believe I was meant to spend my time with them doing work and learning about myself and my ability to handle different jobs.

In time, I would soon know who Mr. Keogh was. Mrs. Keogh always referred to him as the Judge to me. He was hard working right from the start, putting himself though law school. The Judge served as US Attorney in the Eastern District. His military service to his country was honorable and he was awarded the Order of the British Empire for distinguished service to the Allied cause in World War II while in the US Navy. Later, he was distinguished as the Honorable J. Vincent Keogh, New York State Supreme Court Justice. By the time I came around to mow their lawn, I just knew him as Judge K, and missed the swagger and pride of this once powerful man. Back in the day, he was so respected and feared in his field. I am sure he was making a fine salary then, as the place they lived now started as off their summer home.

He had a brother, Eugene James Keogh, who was a Democrat and member of the United States House of Representatives from New York. He was a ranking member of the powerful House and Ways Committee and was involved with sponsoring tax legislation, one becoming the Keogh Plan, a tax shelter plan for small business. When John Kennedy ran for president, Eugene helped him with the New York delegation and in doing so, locked up the Democratic nomination for the president of the United States. He was also close friends with Joseph Kennedy and RFK. I never met his brother the Congressman, as I don't think he came around after what happened to Judge Keogh. I knew the humble man who now was frail, compassionate, and caring.

John F. Kennedy was sworn in as president and had appointed his brother, Bobby, to become Attorney General. Bobby Kennedy was seen as having the highest integrity and must have felt conflicted on his first prosecution case. The Keoghs were an Irish political influence for the Kennedy family, so prosecuting the Judge put them in a terrible spot. Some wanted to just force him to resign, but in the end they went after Judge Keogh. As they say, let the chips fall where they may, and so United States Attorney General Kennedy directed a full investigation of the Keogh case, which lead to Judge K's indictment. I'm sure he was reluctant, as Bobby was quoted as saying, "Goddammit, I told my brother I didn't want this job."

President Kennedy called Eugene to tell him the news and according to history books, he answered back, "You have to do what you have to do, Mr. President." He never forgave Robert for doing this. There is more written in the book *Bobby and J. Edgar* in a chapter called "Panther Piss" that explains the case that snared the Judge. Judge J. Vincent Keogh was charged with taking a bribe in a complex case that involved a powerful teamster, Anthony "Tony Ducks" Corallo, who later would become one of the five Godfathers of New York. Both he and the Judge received two-year jail sentences, and this instantly put an end to Judge K's career that he had worked so hard to achieve.

The Keoghs were a very proud family, so when this happened, you can imagine the talk and gossip in Great Barrington, a small New England town where everyone knew everyone, or at least that is what they thought. The Keoghs went from the spotlight of the nation to turning out the lights in Great Barrington so no one knew they were home. I felt so bad for them and for how many people shunned them. I would never ever shun these people who were so kind to me. They were somewhere between parents, godparents, and grandparents. They were smart, thoughtful, kind, loving, and at times, firm. If I got a little sloppy at doing trimming or mowing, they would, without being too critical, point out my mistake and of course I would rectify the situation.

The Judge and I had something in common: we both had a story we didn't want to talk about, me with the UFO and he with his case that took him down from New York State Supreme Court Justice. I did talk to him about my UFO encounters, but as little as possible. He just said, I believe you, Tommy, and that was good enough for me. He and Mrs. Keogh were about the only adults I talked to about my encounters, and in time even more subjects. Both were like parents who were so discreet, so kind, and so understanding. They seemed to know just what to say at the right time to build my self-confidence with the jobs they had for me. By challenging and building my skills, I felt like I was both needed and loved by them.

Judge Keogh was able to keep his retirement and live out his good days in our neighborhood. I asked my Mom when I found out if the stories were true, and went to a local library and read the story myself. Although I was a bit shocked as I read the headlines and stories, no mater the headline, it didn't change how I felt about the Judge or Mrs. Keogh. Every week after mowing we would have lunch together. We would talk about different subjects, but never politics; I just would not go there, knowing how painful that time must have been for him and Mrs. K.

Through the years, both he and Mrs. Keogh were so supportive of my self-confidence when working around their house. Every spring I looked forward to another season of projects. I enjoyed the problem solving of the projects and beamed with pride when I completed them. Besides lawn clean up and mowing, I would fix their fence and put on storm windows and a porch covering. I put it up every year in the fall and back down in the spring. Of course, there were always minor repairs and painting to be done.

One Saturday, towards the end of my freshman year at Monument Mountain High School, I was mowing the lawn when Mrs. Keogh came out and was crying. Just seeing the look on her face I knew I was about to get horrible news, and I was right. I could not believe the words I was hearing and my heart sunk. My classmate and close, dear friend, Herby Kay, had died in a car accident. The news literally took my breath away and I felt like I was going to vomit right then and there.

We were classmates, teammates in baseball, and friends as far back as I could remember. We went to the same church and he is in our family photos. I can still picture him at our first communion. I was lucky I wasn't with him that horrible, fateful night. That Friday, the day he died, he told me of his fears. We were having lunch together, I think it was Friday pizza at our school cafeteria. There was a song playing on the Monument Mountain High School radio station that they pumped into our cafeteria for entertainment. I remember what the song was and his reaction to the song with the lyrics *dead on arrival*. I was so creeped out right away by the song and so upset hearing the lyrics. He had fear and tears in his eyes and told me how we both would know how this moment would feel. I left school that Friday and came home just wanting to spend time with my parents; I was so alarmed at what Herby had said to me. I recall getting a call from a very close friend, Mike, asking me what I was doing that night and I just said I was staying home. Me too, I have homework to finish anyways, he said.

Mike was close friends with Herby, too, and sat with us at lunch. We always seemed to sit together, and usually in the same spot. Lunch from that day forward would never be the same, and I dreaded going back to school or to lunch or our algebra class knowing his empty seat would be devastating to see. I just did not know how to deal with this news. Somehow the tragedy happened anyway, even though he had premonitions. I had to understand why this happened to my friend, that he knew bad things, evil things were coming, yet could not take the time to stop them from happening. I had to learn to be strong and overcome the driving force behind these life and death decisions that young teens make. At least, I would try.

That day, Mrs. Keogh told me I didn't have to mow the lawn, but I had already started and so I continued mowing and crying till I was done. It was here at the Keogh's I discovered that, for whatever the reason, I was able to communicate with those who had died. I would hear Herby talk to me for years from one part of the lawn to another section. In my mind I called it Herby's section, and he mowed with me every Saturday after that fateful day. Except my friend, I never knew anyone else besides my Dad and brother who was named Herby. In addition to Herby, there were two other young ladies who communicated with me. I had no idea who they were until I researched who lived here before the Keoghs. Every time I was out near the stone remains of the old silo, I would hear them talking to me. They were very pleasant and never bothered me, they just were wanting to connect to me. They were almost angelic. At the time I wondered, Why me? And I also wondered if my close encounters caused me to have these strange abilities. I wasn't in a hurry to find out, nor did I want to talk about the subject except with a few very close friends.

The Keogh property once belonged to Silas Lester, and his two daughters married and went with Joseph Smith and his followers from then what was a relatively small number to today nearly 16.5 million members of The Church of Jesus Christ of Latter-day Saints. Here on the Seekonk Brook, later called the Alford Brook, Smith had baptized the Lester Girls and my great-great-great-grandma. She, however, wasn't going anywhere, while the Lester girls, who had recently married, were. For me, knowing the leader and founder of a major religion had been in our Warner Family Homestead here in the Berkshires before heading west was amazing.

Unfortunately, one of the Lester girls died on the way, and the second right died after the group got out to Salt Lake City, Utah. It was these young women who communicated with me. Whatever the reason, I wasn't afraid of any of them. Their spirits were of love and compassion, and perhaps they were teaching me from beyond the veil of life. My strange Mormon connection started here, but would not end here by any means. My time with the Keoghs, like so many things in life, went by so rapidly. Judge Keogh's heath began to decline rapidly as well. In those short years, diabetes was attacking his frail body, and before long he had both legs amputated. His mind was strong as ever, as he still read books often and wrote letters. I felt so bad for him and so thankful he still insisted I have lunch with him. From time to time I would push him around the yard in his wheelchair so he got to see the property. I was so sad when eventually Mrs. K said they were going to have the house go to their kids and they were going to move into assisted living housing. It's best for us, Tommy, she said.

That spring before they left, the Judge was now limited to his bedroom. Every Saturday I went to see him before I started mowing. Every once in a while he would have me mail a letter for him. I knew he wanted these letter to be private, otherwise he would have had his wife mail them for him. He would hand me the letter upside down so I would not see who the letter was being mailed to, and said the postage was on and just to mail the letter. He asked if I understood what he was saying. I nodded and said, Yes, of course.

Near the end of their time in their home, Mrs. Keogh asked me to make sure to stop by to see him. Judge K asked me to make sure I mailed a particular letter that day and would I return to confirm I had? Of course I would, and after mowing I went into see him.

He said, Mrs. Keogh is going to see our daughter and will be leaving Saturday morning. Make sure you pin feather the lawn and be done early. He handed me the upside down letter and a twenty dollar bill, and off I went. Not once did I ever look to see who they were being sent to. I trusted him and he trusted me; it was that simple. He always tipped me extra to run these private mailings. I ran all the way back from Great Barrington Post Office to let him know I had mailed his letter. I was sweating profusely as I entered the Judge's bedroom, and he grinned when I told him how I ran all the way back. Judge, I said, I just wanted to make sure I made the post office in time. I went to shake his hand and he held my hand in a long pause and smiled. Thank you, Tommy. You're a good boy, and now nearly a young man, a good kind man at that.

The next weekend, as he said, Mrs. Keogh left early and I was busy mowing and did a great job. I have to say, everything was in perfect order and I was rather proud of the job I had just completed. Still, I felt a sadness, for soon they would be moving and all this extra parental love I was so fortunate to have experienced would be gone. They kind of spoiled me with kindness and that was something I cherished. After finishing and saying goodbye to Judge K, I was about to leave when a big black limo pulled up into the driveway. Oh, this must be his company, I thought, and I prepared to leave.

Six men got out of the big black limo and slowly walked over to me, five of them holding the biggest hand guns I ever seen. Oh, my goodness, I thought. No, no, it was more like, Holy shit! The one they were protecting walked up to me and said, You must be Tommy. Hey, boys, look at this, Tommy is Italian. I must have looked puzzled when he asked because he pointed to my shorts. Isn't that an Italian name?

I had an old pair of gym shorts on that I picked up at the end of school year that were left in the lost and found. Free gym shorts were part of my summer wardrobe. Yes, the last name written on those Monument Mountain Athletic shorts was indeed the Italian name of my soccer friend, Rob Negrini. I had looked up to Rob, not only as an athlete but as a person. He was a fine example of how to conduct yourself as an athlete, both on and off the field.

Looking at these fellows I said, Oh, that. No, no, I'm Irish. I stole them. Of course, I didn't steal them, but I was trying to lighten the extremely tense moment. They all laughed and the boss gave me a playful slap on the face. His paws were the size of an Alaskan grizzly, and no doubt he was tougher than one, too. Then he turned very serious saying, Tommy, my friend will stay with you. We are here to see the Judge. He then asked about the layout of the house and area, like were there any houses behind the Judge's house. I assured him there was nothing for miles behind the house then told him how to reach the Judge. I gave them exact directions of the house's layout. Standing there, I was thinking that I was happy the Judge gave me a heads up on his visitors, but with no disrespect to Judge K, I would have rather missed their visit just the same. That being said, I learned a lot about life that day. The fellow guarding me with that big-ass, cold-as-ice hand gun didn't really need it, but I wasn't about to say that to him. I wasn't saying anything to him. Nada!

Beyond the Stars

Not one word was spoken between us; I never made eye contact with him and I doubt he was looking at me. I didn't want to remember him nor did he want me to hear his voice. If ever asked what he looked like, my answer was, I don't know. His voice? I don't know. They were in with the Judge for what seemed like forever and a day. I am sure it wasn't that long, but just felt that way. Finally, they came out and I was so relieved to see them walk toward the limo; but the boss clicked his fingers and sent his guards to the limo. I want to have a talk with Tommy, he said.

He put his arm around me in a way my grandpa would have. I was so nervous as we sat down out at the same table where the Judge and I had, years before, had our first lunch. No bologna sandwich today. This was serious talk. He wanted to know what I thought was the difference between the so-called Mafia and the government. I thought for a moment, taking a deep breath before answering this very deep question, answering respectfully and truthfully. He just nodded at my answers.

I will be clear, the conversation was private and we will keep it that way; however one thing I can share that he did talk about a little was about deep government. Later, I understood he was referring to the so-called men in black. I always like when something was called the so-called anything. I understood what he was saying, and he went on to say that he feared no senator nor congressman, or even president, but there was a deep part of the government he did fear and I should too. I thought if he feared anything, then perhaps I should as well. He had a way of getting his point across in very few words, giving me a lesson of warnings to watch for in life. From that day forward, I would pay attention to what I would hear on the subject. I was very appreciative of his insight.

Somehow or for some reason, Judge Keogh must have told him about my strange encounters with UFOs, and though I wanted to talk more to this powerful man about the subject, his style was to be brief and to the point. Ya understand? he asked. Yes, Sir, I understand. He also went on to say how the Judge said I was kinder to him than his own children. This moved me so, and I said how much both he and Mrs. Keogh meant to me and that they were like parents and grandparents to me, but he already knew that. He could see this in my expressions and the sadness in my eyes talking about the Judge, and not the fear about him, who he was, or those big-ass hand guns those fellows had.

He had come to pay his respects to the Judge the same way I had, and I very much respected that. Respect mattered to me, and I said to him how when they left that I would remember them till long after they left this earth and had gone to heaven, a promise I kept. He said to me, You are safe, Tommy. May you have a long, happy, and prosperous life. He hugged me and he, the limo, and fellows left, never to be seen again.

I never talked about our conversation or the chance encounter to anyone, not even my parents. Before long, the Judge and Mrs. Keogh had left, too, and I felt an emptiness. A part of my life had now changed forever because of the Keoghs. I remember when Judge K died. At his wake, I went up to the coffin and kneeled down to say a prayer and my goodbyes.

I stood up to leave, only to feel an arm around me. There was Mrs. Keogh to comfort me one last time, and together we cried. With those warm Irish eyes, she smiled at me and said, He loved you, Tommy. I hugged her, barely managing to whisper back as my tears continued to flow, I loved him and you, too, Mrs. K. They would forever be in my heart. I did not judge him and he did not judge me.

Chapter 8

Testing My Beliefs

I was being more careful than ever telling my UFO story. Back home, I had talked to my closest friends, Mike, and his sister, Lorene, along with her best friend Sue Vater. Lorene often would talk to me, but her parents made it clear they were not going to let us date. I just wasn't good enough for them, something that was politely expressed. What the hell did they know, anyways? Us kids were all close in those years, and we often hung out together doing fun stuff like swimming in the Green River in the summer and watching sunsets, or just watching TV or even playing ping-pong. I learned to enjoy everyday life with them and was sad when they went their ways in life and I didn't hear from them anymore.

From time to time, I would tell my story of the encounter, not knowing if they were paying attention. I know Suzzie did, as we still talk from time to time about that historic night. Suzzie married her childhood sweetheart, Wyatt Wheeler, and we were friends with Wyatt's sister, Zoa, as well. Zoa and Suzzie were in my graduating class of 1977. Suzzie and Wyatt have been together as far back as I can remember and are now living in Alaska, along with their granddaughter, Celeste, and a number of dogs. I have always appreciated their support in life and feel blessed we are still close.

There was another family I was close with and I had revealed to them that after having close encounters, I developed some rather strange abilities. I don't know why I opened up to them at the time, but it was out of a budding trust and was meant to be. I had a need to talk about all this and felt a desperation to have someone that I could trust with what I had learned. I leave their name out for privacy reasons and the promise not to talk about what or who they knew. My strange ability of mental telepathy and reading minds was developing, but so was the ability to move objects with my mind. This would sometimes give me headaches and eventually, for the most part, I stopped. Yes, for the most part!

My sixteen-year-old self found that revealing this was not something that young ladies liked to talk about, yet I wanted and needed to talk. Luckily, I had some closer friends and this family to talk to. Of course, they challenged me on whatever I told them. When I made a chandelier spin, they were startled and the youngest even thought it was cool. I don't know about cool, but I would go with the word strange! Eventually, I stopped doing this as it took great concentration and sometimes I would get headaches.

I was told there were special schools for kids with these abilities and years later, found they had a connection to the so-called men in black. Back then the United States government was said to being doing tests, and some were not so nice. A source told me while working in counterintelligence that the Russians were working on mental telepathy, and if the Russians were, then we were as well. All this was part of the Cold War. There was no way I was about to go forward in a program to advance a war cause using this skill. I loved my country, but this was just too much. If this was an extension of MK-Ultra, I didn't know nor did I want to ask!

In some ways, I really did feel like a freak and my goal was to make friends, not to scare them away, so I respectfully declined the offer of the special schools. I thought of my experiences at ten and knew that the mental telepathy I experienced was tied to the mind's ability not only to move objects, but also to communicate without words. To talk without words is the ultimate way of conversing that binds the beings of the universe, but only for those with open minds. We use so little of our abilities, and I wondered just what the limitations to my abilities were. I am sure they did as well.

Years later in conversation, I was told not to talk anymore, and that I knew too much about UFOs and other information. This person's father worked with the so-called men in black, as people referred to them, and they had to move every four to five months. What a difficult life that must have been for them, to be constantly on the move to protect whatever knowledge they were obtaining. So I took the advice and keep most of this to myself.

I recall the time I discovered that I was able to move objects with my mind. I had heard of this, but never thought of even trying to actually move something myself. This sort of just happened one day when I was at the Keogh's after they had moved and they had a guest at their house. I was asked to check on a minor repair and I went into a spare room. There was a mobile. As I stared at it, I thought of the UFO just hovering that night here in Great Barrington, visualizing how the UFO was still, yet parts were spinning in different directions. As I did this in my mind, I could hear that mental telepathy and the mobile began to spin. The outer ring in one direction, the next in the opposite, and the most inner ring spun the same direction as the outer ring. Wow, holy cow, I thought.

A little girl who was staying there with her mom and brother walked in just as I was doing this, and screaming, she ran to her mom, yelling, He is moving the mobile and not touching it! She was a bit startled, that's for sure, but I was more freaked out. What the hell did I just do? After they left the room, of course I tried to repeat this feat, and sure enough I could. No need to try explaining this one, I thought but from time to time, I found myself trying to.

Meanwhile on summer vacation, we were back at Lake Champlain and as a teen, I was able to stay out longer into the night. The cabin we stayed at was right on the water, just up from the beach. Many of us would hang out on the beach at night and look at the stars. Little did I know at the time, some of the Clarke family, who hung out with us and visited Lake Champlain, had a close encounter themselves, and on the same night of September 1, 1969.

I was at ease here on Willsboro Point at Lake Champlain. I could spend time alone when I needed to be alone and had a number of lake friends after that quiet time. I cherished my lake friends over the years and very few knew about my UFO experiences. One who did was a friend at the time who was a bit older than us. We used to hang out and tell stories at his garage apartment. Some stories were Adirondack ghost stories told by Greg, and of course my story of UFOs from time to time.

One day as I walked toward the Buena Vista Beach, Greg called me over to his garage apartment, wanting to ask me something. Tommy, a friend of mine is coming down from Plattsburgh. He will be down on the beach and he needs to talk to you, Greg said. Me? Why? The look in his eyes and his one word answer sent shivers down my spine: UFO. Go talk to him, he just got here.

When I walked down to the beach, I saw a younger man with a short haircut in military khaki-like pants, throwing rocks out into the lake. He looked very agitated, and seemed to be throwing those rocks in frustration. He turned to see me and sat down as I approached him. You believe in UFOs? he asked me. Yes I do, I answered.

Greg said you did. Well, why? he asked, as if I were taking some sort of test. I poured my heart out, telling him my close encounter stories.

How mine were at such a close distance of thirty-five feet that there was no way of mistaking them. They were so close and personal, how could I not believe my own eyes? His eyes were tearing up listening to my story and then he told his.

He was a fighter pilot for the US Air Force, flying out of Plattsburgh Air Force Base and they were on sent up on a mission. This was a time when the Cold War with the Soviet Union was in full force, so when something unknown was coming into United States airspace, they must have had adrenaline flowing during this all-out scramble. He told his story as I listened intently to what he said. The intercept he saw was picked up on radar and permission to fire was asked for and given. There in front of him was a UFO. His description was close to the one I had given him. He had lock on the surreal UFO that was hovering in front of him. He heard mental telepathy saying not to fire his weapon, and just as he was about to fire on the UFO, the craft took off at a rate not know to mankind. It's gone, he reported back and he returned to his Plattsburgh, NY base. It was like it read my mind, he said. Well, yes it did, I answered. I understood the mental telepathy. I was stunned as he continued.

When he got back to his debriefing, he was held up and held up until finally two gentlemen, not in military uniforms but suits, came into the room he was held in. They handed him paperwork and he asked, What is this? It's your statement on what happened today, was their answer. He read what they had written and said, This is not what happened; he was told sign the paperwork or walk out the door. They warned him, If you don't sign and walk out the door, you are out of the Air Force and were never in the Air Force. He didn't believe them and walked, and when he returned the next day to report to his job, his life was over as he knew it. He was not allowed on the base and they took his military ID. He called our mutual friend who sent me to him. Why and how the hell would they do that to him? A military coverup of the truth and for what purpose?

The American people could handle the truth then, and of course they can now. I have complete confidence they can.

I felt awful for him and I put my arm around him as he cried. He loved his country, he loved the Air Force, and he loved his job. His faith in his government and truth was rocked to the core. Right before me was broken man, just because he saw a UFO. Just because at the time, no one wanted others to believe they existed. I thought about my conversation at the Judge's home about deep government, and this was about as deep as I could imagine. The flow of information on this subject was controlled and in time I would try to understand why. At this point in time, the story just brought more questions for me. I felt a sense of fear for the knowledge I held and what I experienced.

The biggest question for me was, Why not just tell the truth and look at these from a scientific viewpoint? Fear is born from the uncertain and deep fear and mistrust is born from hiding the uncertainty of the subject, and our government was doing both. Was this to gain an upper hand on the subject matter over our adversaries? For I am sure they were doing the same thing in their countries.

He stood up and gave me a hug, thanking me for saving him. How did I save you? I asked. Because before I talked to you I was thinking about suicide, he responded. We had a hug and I never saw him again. I don't know why I didn't seek his information; perhaps I was a bit scared of his connection to the government. Whatever the reason I may have had at the time, I was wrong and should have done more to stay in touch with this brave American Air Force pilot.

At the lake, my favorite time of day was spent sitting out at night, just looking at the night sky, so drawn to the twinkling stars and the wonderment of space. I never feared the nighttime anymore, instead wondering what was out there. I could sense there was more to this and one day humans would find that answer.

How is it they reached out to this speck of dust planet and even more, could find me, and why? I began to expand on my Catholic faith, now reflecting on my spiritual side, even at this young age of sixteen. How dare that priest say I had Satan in me, because I knew what happened to me was real. I did not have Satan in me, I had two UFO abduction encounters. I was tagged and was a messenger, but understanding the message would take so many years to comprehend and even more to be brave enough to say. To say I was questioning my beliefs about trusting was an understatement; however, time on Lake Champlain would open and solidify my beliefs and self-confidence.

I not only would look to the stars as a macro view but the very earth we walk upon as a micro view. Within that micro view, I appreciated every aspect of nature. Here, sitting on the end of Willsboro Bay, I would watch every sunset I got a chance to take in. As the sun would fall into the Adirondack Mountains, I found my love of expressing what I saw and turned these thoughts to paper. My craft of poetry was born out of this spirituality. Art and poetry and my love of nature would forever define me and were nurtured by nature and those UFO encounters. I left my self-doubt behind on a worry rock and tossed it off Hatch Point, deep into the waters of Lake Champlain.

When we share the feelings of nature and put those words to paper, we learn to share our soul. Your heart beats because you have a soul. No heart, no soul; no soul, no heart. They are the necessary parts of a symbiotic relationship for human existence. Listening to the gull cry from above, I realized the answers to life were more than the possessions you accumulate or the hight of power you may reach. I was a poor lad, and yet I could enjoy the very sunset palette before me just as much as the rich person passing by on his yacht.

There was another reason I was so drawn to this spot at Willsboro, Lake Champlain. It's a feeling that has always been so difficult to explain. My senses were like an antenna beacon to supernatural experiences. A connection, if you will, to a far off source not from this earth, but at sixteen I was not willing to talk about these feelings. I would just go about my life as a young athlete, spending hours juggling a soccer ball to hone my skills for the chance to be a professional player. The long runs to get in shape were my private time out in nature. I would run everywhere and on my runs, the nagging question was not far behind. What the heck was I sensing? The answer always came back to my close encounters as a child, which took me years to accept and to believe.

Think of the subject this way: you watch the movie *Jaws* and the movie is placed in your memory. If something triggers that memory, you can pull up that John Williams theme song, knowing that big shark is not far behind that poor young girl who is skinny dipping, feeling the warm summer New England air. I remember seeing that movie at the famous Mahaiwe Theater in Great Barrington, and as I watched a scene, dropping my popcorn in fright. This is our capability as humans to have a memory and recall that memory at will.

Our own life experiences, too, are a treasure trove of recorded memories through experiences, and a gift to share. We share our stories of our life's journey by recalling the memories. My life is no different, except on one level.

While I recall my life in memory, this rewind, if you will, of my life movie also includes a second recall of another life. This recall all started after my close encounters, and they are of a far off place and time, and definitely another planet. I can see this earth like a place where I lived. A small town on a lake with a beach. Perhaps this is the reason I was so drawn to Lake Champlain. The lake was similar to the memories etched in me of a world far away.

The transportation on this world was vehicles that floated just above the ground. The one part of this far away planet that stood out the most was communication through mental telepathy. This was the same type of telepathy that brought me out of the Shaw house, running frantically that night of September 1, 1969. Now at sixteen, I was getting messages from beyond our earthy bounds and my challenge was to understand those messages. I felt there were two distinct themes given as old and repeating as are the galaxies we watch in the night sky.

Beyond the Stars

There are two forces in the world, two opposing energies, one to destroy the other. You could say good and evil, or right from wrong, but for me they encompass the difference between life or death as well. The journey would continue or end depending on how I listened to these messages. As I confided to a few close to me, it only drew a wedge between these friendships. My youth was guided by a belief that the force looking out for me was that of goodness and love. My very being was to love and be loved, and my entire life has been that focus, not just with people but with the nature of this earth as well. My weakness as a human was my failure to listen as I tried to block out these messages.

The lessons would get more dangerous till I became a believer in the vast worlds of the universes. Though we are just a speck of sand, our importance never can be overlooked nor underestimated. A sandy beach is nothing without the endless individual grains of sand, just as our importance to humanity is our own existence; we are those individual grains. We as individuals make up humanity, all of us different yet part of that same planet we call earth. My spiritual being was now growing in part by those around me and a spiritual force I would come to know, proving to me that the force could prevail in my world.

Daniel Warner and sons, Henry and William J. in 1853

Warner Homestead tennis court and barn in 1921

Ma with Clan Warner

Dad fishing

Bo, John, Tommy, and Delphine Bean

Little Tommy trying to get in the picture in 1961

Grandpa Will Warner

Lottie Warner

Bo and Tommy getting ready for church

Christmas 1964

First Communion

Ten-year-old Tommy

Grandma Shaw and Mom

Tough times for Judge K

Warner Swimming Hole at Seekonk Brook

Mom and Dad

Swimming in the middle of Lake Champlain

Eighteen-year-old Tom Warner

In GUG we trust

Who ever gave you that note knows way to [sic] much

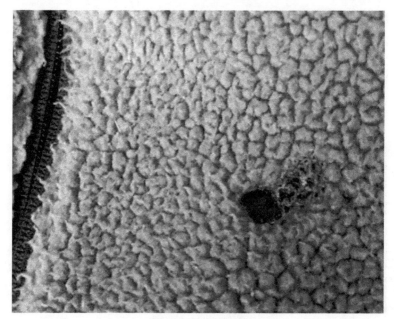

The burned coat

Tom with Civil Rights Leader Dr. Lenora Taitt-Magubane

Tom filiming *Unsolved Mysteries*

Thank you to all involved!

Thank you for sending the beautiful giclee entitled Five Acres. It is a striking, visual record of James Weldon Johnson's connection to New England. It will have a place of honor in Emory University's James Weldon Johnson collection. Thanks for your generous gift and for keeping alive the memory and achievement of a great American: James Weldon Johnson.

- Rudolph P. Bird, Founder,
James Weldon Johnson Institute, Atlanta, Georgia

Chapter 9

Life or Death and My Guardian Angel

Now in my seventeenth year here on planet Earth, my thoughts turned to what I was going to do with my life. I suppose that was because schools push what you are going to do with your future. My goal at seventeen was to be a professional soccer player and I so looked forward to my senior year at Monument Mountain here in Great Barrington. I loved the feeling of playing this sport as well as the friendships that I had while being on a team. To be successful, you had to have everyone on the same page.

Two years prior, we had an undefeated JV team, and the varsity team won the state championship. The next year we placed second, so I was more than ready to make my mark and move forward my senior year. A great senior year would perhaps lead to some scholarships, not just in soccer but by getting good grades as well. I was a decent B+ student, but hell, I had an A in soccer and I knew it. I had the strength in my kick that was above normal as all those days of endlessly kicking a ball against a wall were paying off. As a fullback, I once scored on a direct kick beyond forty yards out. My dear coach, Larry Webb, said I had a thundering shot and could use both legs shooting. I was well-balanced, knowing that the center of my being was my very soul.

By my senior year, I had finished my college prep courses and I was allowed to take an art course. Work First, was Mom's only requirement. I missed those art classes and I chose a pottery class, as I had an idea for a new art form. The idea came from Kenny and Jon Aronoff's piece that hung in the hall of our beloved Monument Mountain High School. The piece covered a large space and was above the entrance to the auditorium. I so looked up to the two athletes who had done the piece, as they were good friends and teammates of my older brother, Mike. Mike was a hell of a soccer player himself and left big shoes for all three of us younger Warners to follow.

I spoke of the Arnoffs earlier and wanted to add how much I looked up to them, not only as soccer players but also how kind they were. Being the youngest, I was so appreciative of both of them for their constant kindness. Jon went on to be Dr. Jonathan Aronoff, a licensed psychologist, certified personal and executive coach, psychoanalyst, sports coach, and certified group fitness instructor. Kenny went on to became one of the most famous drummers in the world and has been voted top 100 drummers of all time. For years he was the drummer for John Mellencamp, and later in his famous career was the drummer for *The Night That Changed America: A Grammy Salute To The Beatles*. Today, Kenny is a motivational speaker and he lives his life by example. They gave me a spark to do art as well as sports, something I will always be grateful for and appreciative of.

As much as everything was looking up, I began to have premonitions that I was in danger. As every one of these events happened, I began to pay attention, but concern turned to worry. School had let out and I had my lawns to take care of for spending money. Early summer meant endless days at the Green River with my close friends Mike, Lorene, Suzie, and Wyatt.

These were some of the same spots where William Cullen Bryant would walk and write. This famous poet would write about the river so green, and there are many places you can see this today. Word was that he walked this river and the Alford Book, perhaps spending time in thought or taking time to walk to his true love's home in Alford.

The spot where we hung out was called the pumping station, where the town of Great Barrington drew its water supply from. The water was never warm, but always refreshing. You didn't really swim in the Green River; it was more like in and out then warm up, as the water was cold enough to chill penguin. You could always count on that refreshing and very alive feeling after a dip.

Many times after being at the Green River, we would sit watching the sunset on a ridge up from the river. The vast Berkshire views from that ridge meant you could see the entire Seekonk vista all the way to the now well-known Berle Sheep Farm. Then at night, we would watch the skies to look for falling stars. From time to time, I would talk about my UFO encounters while looking at the night sky, but that summer I began to talk about how I felt danger. On one hot summer night, I heard that voice telling me there was danger. I told Mike that we had to be fast going for a swim and that the sky would light up after he dove in. I just went under for a quick cool off and got out, and sure enough, Mike dove in and heat lightning went off. In that moment, for a brief flash, nighttime turned to day. Mike shot out of that water like it was a cannon. Strange things like this happened all that summer of 1976, even while on summer vacation on Lake Champlain. As the summer went on and we got back from Lake Champlain, soccer started back up, but I felt an awful emptiness.

Lorene started dating a friend of mine. For years I could talk to her about my thoughts of life, and now her and her brother, who I had considered my best friend, had become distant. I think he sensed something was going to happen, too. On the soccer pitch, I turned to my teammate, Wally, and said, Wally, I have to go back up to the lake. So that night I arranged to go back up to Willsboro by the Amtrak 69, not knowing my fate was sealed for another Labor Day encounter.

That weekend I stayed with friends of mine, just hanging out at the beach and having some Miller Beers while we talked about the upcoming school year. The weekend was going by fast and the next day we would all depart for the year. The feeling was that we were moving on slowly from our youthful days to adulthood. We would laugh and say that we would write to each other, knowing full well that we rarely would. Now, had we had the Internet back then, perhaps that would have been a different story. Sure, about every Christmas I would get a short note in the cards we sent. We were lake friends and some I have to this day.

Sunday was here now and after going for a swim, I just wanted to be by myself. I was feeling empty inside and felt that the alone feeling had more to do with a past life than the one I was living. This feeling was overwhelmingly intense.

As the sun went down, I walked to a place on the Willsboro Bay where the boats launched. That summer, we gathered there night after night, but by now the summer people had gone home and only the last few remained. Summer was moving on now to fall. I sat on a wall that faced the setting sun and gazed at the sky as the colors faded and the night stars appeared one by one. In my peripheral vision, I saw a young lady appear. I did not see where she came from and I remember her like it was yesterday. She wore a distinctive jacket and had long, light brown, flowing hair. Her eyes were mesmerizing as she looked at me and came closer and spoke. I miss my two sisters and brothers, she said in a sad voice. What happened to them? I asked. She said, Not them. Me. I died a year ago to this date. You are in grave danger and you must listen to my voice. LISTEN TO MY VOICE. Years later I would learn her name and all about her life.

Just then, I heard a friend call to me off in the distance. I ran up to him and he asked what I was doing. I answered that I was talking to that girl. Tom, I didn't see anyone, are you OK? he asked. Yeah, I answered, but I'll catch up with you guys later. The girl was gone as soon as I turned to go back to the wall. This was the first encounter with this spirit, but would not be my last. Slowly, I started walking back to the Buena Vista Beach. I felt a tug similar to when I was ten and my arms went back with that UFO. My attention was drawn to the sky, and looking up I saw something startling, as startling as the UFO the first time. As I looked to the northeast night sky, I saw a porthole in a triangle formation. I could feel energy coming from the porthole and it was so strong, I felt like it could pick me up off the ground. I felt fear and could sense danger, and more than ever before, to say I felt terrified would be an understatement. Was this to a different dimension? I just didn't know.

After getting back, we all decided to stay at one house with no supervision for a bunch of drinking teen boys. This spelled trouble right from the start. I don't know why we drank so much that night, but we did and of course, alcohol makes for horribly bad decisions. I went to bed early and drunk. Someone woke me up to go to town and being half awake, my fate was set for disaster.

It was after 2 AM, and going to town we almost hit a telephone pole. Then the driver did a doughnut in a parking lot, almost crashing into a building. At that moment I fell asleep and I lost time. How much time could be debated. The next thing I knew, I woke to a hard bump coming from the left side of the car, as if the car were hit from the side, and my eyes opened. Sitting in the middle up front, I glanced to see the speedometer was over 100 mph. I knew in fraction of a second that I was facing death, and again time went into very slow motion. At this moment, I also had a vision of a UFO.

We were going backwards at 100 mph and time was going one frame at a time. The first hit was sideways as we slammed into the stone wall with such force, then back off the wall as we went for a second go at death. The second hit to the wall felt like being punched by a Muhammad Ali left hook all over my body, and yet the car backed off the wall again. The third time into the wall, the car went on top of the wall and we hit a boulder, shooting the car end over end, and the last of the fading lights told me we were above the trees.

Yes, what goes up must come down, and we came down with such devastating force. We were tossed like rag dolls and by some miracle, I was flat as the car made the most awful noise you could ever imagine. I could taste the metal of the now crushed car as it was pounded into pavement mixed with busted glass. Everything met in that moment when my world went black and I was knocked unconscious. When I woke, I was so surprised I had survived and thought it must be daylight as I was starting to see a little light. Little did I know it was 5 AM and the light I was seeing was not a pleasant sunrise but rather the car starting to burn. Oh, my God, I thought, We are on fire, we have to get out.

When I say panic set in, I mean panic set in, instantly, right away. I could not believe that I had survived the crash and was now about to die trapped in a burning car. I was about to be burned alive. With my life flashing before me, my mighty soccer legs were kicking the door in front of me with all my might, but to no avail. I went through the stages of grief from denial, to anger, bargaining, depression, and finally acceptance. When I reached acceptance, I left my body and now was viewing the burning car from above. Shit, shit, shit, I thought. I saw from above that the driver's door was open. The door behind me was open the whole time but I could not see it because I could not turn my head; viewing the car after leaving my body meant I could see.

Just then the voice of the girl from the boat launch said, The door. I want to go back, I told her. You are, she responded, and in that instant I was back in the burning car, but now I knew the way out. I wiggled and wiggled to get to that open space and sat up outside the car, and saw a guy named Nang had also gotten out. That left my good buddy, Steve, still in there. I was confused why Nang did not get me out because when I got out, he was just standing there. As I stood up, I thought I had lost my left arm, but I had not. I was just holding it against my chest, protecting my now broken arm. The pain was mind-boggling, enough to make you puke. And I did want to puke.

We have to get Steve out, I said and I was shocked to hear Nang say, He's too far gone. My mind was going as fast as that car was. Why would he say that? Fuck you, I said, No one dies tonight if I can help it. I made Nang help me and we pulled Steve out. After he was out, I hid behind a boulder as the car exploded and flames shot high into the air. The rush and confusion now was replaced by the delight of hearing the screaming sirens of fire trucks and an ambulance coming to our aid. I never knew who it was who found me behind that boulder, but they knew who I was. Oh, my God, it's Tommy Warner.

We were rapidly put in the ambulance. I heard the radio call from the New York State Police, This in NYSP. You have have escort and clearance to CVPH. I-87 will be cleared, I repeat 87 will be cleared. I kept telling myself over and over, No way this ambulance could crash, no way this ambulance could crash. We went very, very fast on that interstate, all the way to Plattsburgh. The next I heard was our condition: one serious, one critical.

I talked to Steve the whole way and when we got to the ER they kept me nearby, saying he was responding to my voice. I was told I talked nonstop for nearly an hour. The next thing I remember was talking to my mom just before I was going into surgery. We all survived that night and after recuperating from our surgeries, we all made it back home to our families. That Labor Day weekend that I listened to that voice was the introduction to my guardian angel.

Chapter 10

Who Do I Talk To?

After a successful surgery to put my broken arm back together and a week or so in Champlain Valley Physicians Hospital in Plattsburgh, my parents arrived to take me back home. We stopped in Willsboro to take pictures of the mangled and flattened car, the death trap that only a guardian angel could have pulled me from. I thought of Nang and why he watched me struggle, so near death. The thought was as cold as a pile of ice-cold steel. Dad took a few picture then started to cry. He wrapped his arms around me and we did not say a word, for nothing more needed to be said. We took our time that day, taking the slow but scenic Route 22 south, making sure to stop for Mom at Roma Restaurant in Whitehall. Three gyros to go with chips and Mountain Dews. Mom and Dad knew how to brighten up even the worst moments. Perhaps a bit of food for comfort, something we all needed at that time.

Upon arriving home, reality set in rather fast that school had been in session and I still was not up to going. The twins, Bo and John, were off to college at Keene State and now it was just Mom, Dad, and I at home. The silence was refreshing at first, but I could tell Mom and Dad missed having them around. This was the beginning of good bonding time, even though I was not opening up about the accident much or that guardian angel. My sadness was just awful.

Mom, who was a nurse at our local Fairview Hospital, was more like a doctor at home, setting my time for recovery to one more week. Her concern was that I would not be able to catch up on my classes, but that was never a concern for me. Every day I kept waiting for teammates to call, or even friends. No one called or showed up that week, and my heart sunk like the Titanic. At first I would go to my room and cry, feeling sorry for myself, but after a while it did no good and I had to start looking to myself for answers. The night before going back to school, two classmates finally did stop by for a minute with school books and assignments. Oh, gee, I thought, school books. Thanks! Mentally and physically I was not prepared to go back to school, but Mom said it was time for me to get back on the horse and go. Her motto of Dust Yourself Off did make sense and so I did.

Not one of my teammates stopped by to check on me, and that bothered me for some time. Gone was my soccer year, and any hopes for an athletic scholarship were gone as well. I made every effort to return that fall of 1976 to play for my high school, but the danger of reinjuring my arm put that out of reach. All of us, me, my parents, and my coach, knew this, but I was hard-pressed not to try. Sadly, try I did, but to no avail; there was just no way of a comeback, not for this season.

All that preparation, hours of working out and mile after mile of running, gone in one night of poor decisions. After high school, I would continue my craft of this fine sport of soccer, both playing and teaching. I came close to turning professional as a player and was the youngest coach hired by Puma All Star Soccer Schools. The academy by Puma was the first in the nation, and it was an honor to teach with perhaps the greatest legendary technical coach the game has ever had in Hubert Vogelsinger. Years later, my career would end for good with an eye injury.

I loved the game of soccer and how playing made me feel about myself, both as an athlete and person.

My efforts and concentration would now have to be on my grades and my newfound love of art. Mom wanted and insisted that college prep courses be done before art courses. She knew how to motivate us Warner boys; work before play was how she saw it. I was thrilled to have a theatre course and even be in a play. I wasn't going to be in theatre, but it did give me the opportunity to appreciate all the hard work of that art form and I got to be in *The Lion, the Witch, and the Wardrobe.* Years later I would be fortunate to meet greats in this field and see the work they did, and knowing how difficult this trade was, I appreciated their craft from a distance.

The most important course for me, though, was ceramics with Irishman John ffrench. I never knew this man's great talent and often wonder if the students then knew of his brilliance in his field. He encouraged my understanding and perception of the medium of clay and using that medium as a visual art, instead of as practical use in pottery. What are you doing? he would first ask. Painting with my fingers and soul, I answered. Rather than say you can't do that, he said, Great, that is lovely, keep going. I can still hear his voice to this day. He encouraged me just as Norman Rockwell, another great and famous Stockbridge artist, had years before. Norman's fame went so far into the world and touched so many of our lives, both us Berkshire neighbors and of course the world. Tommy, he said, If you're going to paint a picture, have it tell a story. Otherwise, don't bother painting. I took his advice to heart.

Well in our family, a raconteur always emerged, passing on our family stories from the 1600s on Nantucket Island to our 1835 Warner Homestead. Here in my art class I was doing this in a new way, doing scenes in 3D clay, firing the piece in a kiln and using earth tone colors to create a painting. Someone must have loved my work, as every piece was stolen upon completion. Every one of those pieces told a story. I wonder if whoever stole my pieces knew or if they understood the UFO implications I hid in every piece.

The only piece that survived was a bowl that everyone had to make. The bowl was a slip piece and you got to decorate it. Mine was a combination of both forces in the universe, some earthy and some not. It had symbols that I drew with no idea where I saw them. They were UFO images and mystical images shown to me, such as the triangle porthole. Mr. ffrench liked the piece but said he would prefer never to have a snack from that! I was just trying to express my thoughts on what I had been through and didn't bother to try and explain myself, nor the mysterious symbols I had seen.

Back then I thought, Where would I ever begin? That young woman, my guardian angel, and talking to her was still etched in my mind, just like the UFO. I also couldn't shake the image of the strange triangle porthole shown to me, where I could feel the energy pulling on me. Why was I drawn to the Willsboro Bay so strongly in the first place? Answers are only as good as the questions asked. If you ask the right question, then perhaps you will find the right answers, and at the time I just did not have the right questions.

The more I tried to block the spiritual side of nature out, the more it all would come to me in my dreams. Some of them were good, but some were the awful flashbacks of that crash. I just kept having those nagging questions, Why would someone want me to burn alive, and how did that spirit find me and save me? Was she connected to that porthole, and if so, how? I felt like the porthole was connected with my close encounters. Perhaps I would just let it all go and forget about it, talking only to that voice within me. For at eighteen, there was not really anyone to talk to who would believe me anyway.

Chapter 11

Save Me From My Teens

Well, lo and behold, I graduated after that tumultuous senior year and enrolled at Berkshire Community College. Everyday life was changing now that I turned eighteen and I was encouraged by my parents to look to the future of what I wanted to do. I was prepared to study business administration and then go on to a four year college. Oh, such a great plan, except that was the last thing I really wanted to do. My heart was still set on getting back to soccer.

All was going well that summer, until one night I found myself in a bad situation again. I was at our Buena Vista Beach when the New York State Police broke up a summer party. Rather than walk home, just four houses down from the Buena Vista Beach, I hopped in a car with some strange kids. I have no idea who they were, and I figured we were going to ride around the park and come back; but instead we drove to another town and ended up parked in a field. The driver knew where he was and his attitude was controlling to all that were there. His friends asked what we were doing there and he just laughed. I had a slight feeling of danger.

At that point, I heard a familiar voice, the same one that I heard at the boat launch the year before. By now the driver had started drinking and smoking strong weed, and I knew I had to leave and find my way back home. I walked away down this dark, forest-lined dirt road, not knowing which direction to go. The coyotes howling in the distance were not much comfort, as perhaps they would see me as easy prey. Maybe not easy, but prey just the same. Eventually, the old dirt road opened up to where I could see the sky. The August weather was a bit crisp for that time of year, which meant the sky was clear. Looking up, I saw a shooting star and made a wish, and the next thing I saw was not what I was wishing for. That same triangular porthole appeared in the sky. My pounding heart just about jumped out of my chest and I was so scared.

I was saying to myself, You will be OK, you will be OK. Just keep walking. But then I would look up to see it was still there. The third time I looked, it was gone; but what was it that I saw? The energy I felt coming from the sky was indescribable, other than it gave the same feeling as I had the split second that I saw the UFO back in 1969. At any moment I thought a UFO would descend upon me. Singing John Denver's "Country Roads" distracted me, till off in the distance the beautiful sight of Lake Champlain appeared. Knowing where I was gave me comfort, but having six more miles to get back to our summer home was awful.

My thoughts of my mother worrying about my whereabouts were overwhelming. As luck would have it, my good friends came looking for me. One of the teens who was in that car in the woods knew who I was, and after getting to his house went back to tell my friends that I took off and was missing. I was so happy to get back and told a close friend about what I had seen in the sky. The look he gave was like I had lobsters crawling out of my ears, but after awhile I got a scared confirmation of belief.

The next night, I was at a party at a friend's house. My plan was just to walk home, but when I walked outside, there was my guardian angel again. From that moment on, my decisions were like a blur and, of course, I was with good friends and had another car accident. To this day I feel so bad about what my poor decisions put my parents through.

When my Dad picked us up from the Smith House, the local clinic, the look on his face was of worry and relief at the same time. I still had to face Mom, and that was almost more than I could bear. Mom's words were quick and short: Just look at yourself in the mirror and decide how you want to keep living your life. Your so-called friends and you are living a dangerous life. You will die if you don't change.

I went to bed in terrible pain with a banged up knee that I had declined treatment for. I had a message in a dream that perhaps I should be punished and have all my golden blond locks fall out. I sat up like a submarine on an emergency blowout of water. With such a start, I hobbled with a limp to the mirror and ran my hand through my blond locks, only to see them start falling out.

Ahhh, oh, my God, I called, like I was five years old, and Mom came in so fast because she could hear the panic in her little boy's voice. At that moment, I was indeed a little helpless and humble boy. I told her of my dream and much to my relief, Mom was grinning as she examined my head. She said, Tommy, you're not losing your hair, you are coved in small pieces of glass and it is cutting your hair. She cleaned out the shards of tiny glass then had me wash my hair and sent me off to bed to try to sleep.

I went to bed for the night. I was alive and thankful, but more than that, I learned that I really did have a guardian angel who would be my spirit guide throughout my life. A guide is someone who shows you the way but does not judge you. We are imperfect because we are human, gifted with free will when tested.

The test of my beliefs came just over one week later. I was in bed for a few days and thought, I have to just walk a little to get this rust out of my swollen knee. Of course, I knew this was a setback again for soccer, and rest for me meant being on the beach, listening to the waves, and contemplating life itself. The now-cooling water of Lake Champlain felt so good on my sore knee. In about five days the pain let up, so walking very short distances was fine. All my friends told me they were planning a sleep out at the mouth of the Bouquet. The Bouquet River started way up in the Adirondack Mountains and emptied into Lake Champlain. At the mouth was a very sandy beach. No, thanks fellas, was my answer.

Oh, yes, the frontal lobe of a teen brain not yet developed till early twenties. I was rather proud to say no, thanks. Wow, how mature of me. This part of the brain for decision making, including impulses, had not gotten the best of me. At eighteen, I may not always have made the most logical decisions and some were downright dumb, as Dad would tell me. Never did I think it was because of my youthful brain not going through a logical process to reach a logical conclusion about danger.

Despite this good decision, I would fail and be susceptible to peer pressure in the sense of fitting in and hanging with friends. Friendship meant so much to me and we had so many good times and laughs in our youth that it was hard to say no to them all. I knew this all had to stop, and in doing so, it would signal a change in my journey to move forward on the spiritual journey that was calling me.

That late afternoon, they all took off in boats with sleeping bags and enough food and snacks to last a week. I didn't even mention their planning a sleep out to my parents, and that evening I went to the beach to just look to the lights of Burlington and the stars above. Content to listen to the lapping waves and watch the reflection of the far-off city lights, I felt a sense of peace till that voice of my guardian broke my visualizing trance. Your friends will need you. They will come for you and you will save them. Have faith that you can do this, she said. This was the last thing I wanted and part of me wanted to run away. Forget being a hero! Why do I have to be a hero anyway? But I loved my friends and if this was the case, I had to be brave and show no fear.

Off in the distance I could see the port and starboard lights approaching, and I can still hear the familiar voices to this day. Billy T helped guide the eighteen-foot boat in to the beach. Dave was driving his family's boat, along with three other friends. We had to get more stuff, someone yelled. Billy added, Hey, Tommy, we're not drinking. I swear to God we're not drinking. Come on and have a sleep out. Oh that recognizable Yonkers New York accent that aways brought a smile to all our faces! I went home and told my parents, and they said it was fine, as long as there was no drinking. With that we were off!

As we left the shore, I was on edge, right from the start of that motor. I was watching the driver, Dave, like a hawk, and he was being careless as he drove this powerful boat. Put your damn hands on that steering wheel, I said. Don't be a pussy, Warner, he answered. And at that moment we hit a rogue wave and he lost control of the boat. Instantly, time went still for me, just like in other life or death situations, and because of this I was able to react. From my childhood experience of falling through an icy brook to this moment facing a certain ending, it had been ingrained in my being to react to time slowing from seconds to milliseconds.

In that second, from the back seat I dove for the steering wheel, catching it and throttling back, all in one motion as Dave was thrown back out of the driver's seat. Will you listen to me now? I yelled. Had I not caught the wheel, the boat would have flipped over. My ordeal was over and I passed another test of courage, bravery, and love for my friends. Holy shit, my good friend, Jeff Lasher, yelled. I could see Jeff's head was wet as he had hit the water; the boat was that close to going over at such a high rate of speed.

All six of us could have died, but we didn't on that night. And had I not gone, five would have died for sure, and I would have been left thinking, Why didn't I go to help save them? Nothing more needed to be said as everyone understood the gravity of what just happened, and we all knew we wanted to put it behind us right away. There was only a little discussion when we arrived safe and sound to the sandy beach at the mouth of the Bouquet. I just put out my sleeping bag by the fire and was so happy to be enjoying hot dogs and s'mores. I asked, Hey, guys, is there a wanted poster of me dead or alive in the post office? Cause if not, can we stop doing this?

A few jokes were said and we were so thrilled with where we were in the moment that the time passed quickly. We ate lots of junk food and cooked some marshmallows. I was so happy we were all safe. With the incredibly soft sand beneath us, I was so content and looked at the stars above on the clearest of nights, without a cloud in the sky. I stayed up so late, looking out into the night sky till the embers on the campfire faded and all my friends had long since ended their conversations and fallen into a deep slumber.

My slumber would wait, but the repetition of the lapping waves eventually took me to a deep, peaceful, safe night's sleep. Not till the early morning sunrise was I startled awake, as Lake Champlain, so calm just hours ago, was now choppy and would challenge us boys, for it was time to leave this teen utopia.

Dave's family boat did not start right away and I rode back with my buddy, Mark Bertino, in his aluminum boat with an exterior motor. As we bounced, hitting every wave, with water splashing on us, Mark laughed. This is living! he yelled. Hanging on as we went and feeling the Lake Champlain water splash my face, I answered, Yes, it is Mark. Yes, it is.

This was the last time I spent with my teen group. Oh, sure, some of us would stay in touch and even reconnect in the social universe of Facebook. But here on this beach, on this August summer day, we parted as a group. We all agreed to keep the story hush for the time being about our adventure, and for me, well, I was moving on from my teens, saved and thankful to be alive. I was now open to so many thoughts that there was more to the universe than meets the eye and more to spirituality than meets the soul. I was given a gift that few are given to communicate telepathically both with humans and beyond. There, on that boat ride back to Willsboro Point with my dear friend Mark, this all became clear to me, and saying anything to anyone would do no good. In time, I would question all this, but proof of existence would be shown when needed.

Chapter 12

Another Planet, Another Life

Ten years after the UFO descended upon me in Great Barrington, I began to think about the repeated visions I was having. My thoughts echoed from childhood to my teen years to early adulthood. There are reasons why I have these dreams and visions. To me, there was a difference between a dream and a vision. A vision is clear and precise, whereas dreams are mixed, though meaningful, thoughts and experiences, like a puzzle. In some of my dreams, I would have flashbacks. Yet other times I would recall visions of a room on the UFO where I could get glimpses of strange surroundings and the others that were there. The one girl I remembered so well with a panicked look in her eyes haunted me. The look of complete fear screamed out with just her eyes. That image is forever embedded in my memory.

Remembering the panic in her eyes, and knowing no words were needed, connected us on that UFO in that moment in time. As much as her eyes were begging for help, I, too, was helpless. My memory was of taking in the sights I could, such as colors and seeing a table and also seeing the colored lights. Colors I had not seen before, yet were very distinctive, just the same. There is just no way to reproduce them, not even for me as a watercolor artist.

When in high school at Monument Mountain in Great Barrington, I was walking down the hall and opened the door, and in an instant my breath was taken away. There she was, right in front of me, and I remembered those eyes that could talk to you. I felt my heart race in panic as I had an instant flashback of being on that UFO. As the chills went down my spine and the hairs on my arm stood up, I had to find out who she was and if in fact it was her on that UFO. I could not just ask, but finding out who she was no big deal.

Her connection to the UFO on that September 1, 1969, would take a back seat for now. I turned around and followed her, and then asked someone outside her class what her name was. Melanie, came the answer. Many years would pass, more than forty-five years, before I learned of her whole story, but her family story was told to me in high school. They were the family at Lake Mansfield that fateful night.

Back to the vision I was consistently having of another planet. This vision of another planet is perhaps the most difficult to write about or even explain, mostly because it was the most difficult part for me to come to grips with; and yet I have so many visions that I hold of this place. Knowing how bizarre this sounds to the average person does not make it easier to write. I feel compelled to tell the story because of the meaning the vision has in the overall story. Everything was connected, from the mental telepathy as a young child, to being abducted twice in a two-week period, and event after event.

The hardest part of the story to tell was that I was given a vision of having once lived on another planet, and the reason for this knowledge was so that others would know there is more out there and that we are connected. How the hell did they get there? is the question I grapple with, but I have a few theories for later in the book. My memory recall shows me in a past life on distant planet, living in a small town.

The planet's surroundings are very much like those here on earth. This idea of a different life, as in a past life, is so bizarre and yet I know it happened. The town sits on a cove on a rather large lake. It has a beach with a raft in the water along with boats on their moorings to both sides. There are mountains in the distance.

The cars that are driving by have no wheels, but float above the road. I lived right up the hill from this spot, overlooking the lake, and there are times I can recall what this looks like. My life there is like a film, and the most important memories are those feelings of being loved. Seeking and needing the emotion of unconditional love is what drives me as a human being. Being loved is the most important human emotion and never can be taken for granted. Being loved truly, unconditionally, is the closest to perfection that any being can experience, and reaching for that is forever in my heart and soul. Here on a planet so far away, visions of a life were put in me on that September 1, 1969, night.

As painful as it was to recall, this all had a purpose and my connection to that time and place must have meaning. I was shown true love, unconditional love, for both people, planet, and galaxy. All are necessary in their respect for each other in order to continue their existence. The same is true with this planet and for our own existence. From time to time, I would be shown examples of this here on earth as a reminder that anything is possible, including mental telepathy. There was one constant in that telepathy that started when I was just a child: the one who communicates is the same all through these years. Never say never, always say forever. From galaxy to galaxy, through all time and space, anything is possible.

My feeling was that the metal telepathy, where words are not needed in conversation but are transmitted by a thought process, made language unnecessary. The one who communicates would also warn of dangers to me and when I would meet new people, would point out those that had a direct correlation to my journey in life. There was a clear difference between the one communicating via mental telepathy and my guardian angel. I later came to know who she was, and who her wonderful family members were. So what do I mean by that?

That mental telepathy communication from beyond never went away and continues to this day. My guardian angel comes around just to straighten out my off-course butt! I clearly listen to both and always have. Be with people who will listen, not just with their ears, but also with their hearts. When necessary, I would sense danger and I would sense fear as lessons in life. I was born with this perplexing gift, and it took me most of my life to appreciate this valuable insight. I do not fear life on other planets, but embrace those memories given to reach out to others.

In my short life, I had been through so much, to the point that fear was almost a normal part of seeing events happen before they actually happened. Not only this, but the real scary part for me was that I could communicate with people who had passed on. Come on, that is creepy to think about, even for me, till you realize that it is talking to a different dimension in time. There we go again, talking about time; perhaps we need to rethink time. Life is time and is measured and defined by humans with the understanding that their capability is limited to both time and space. Like my life here and there, both blended into forming who I have become.

Not only would I see events before they happened, but the same happened with people I saw prior to meeting them. I would know when I was about to meet someone before I met them, and sure as the sun would rise, I would meet them. This always made me begin to think about the perplexing definition of time. See, we think of time in seconds to minutes to hours to days and so on, but what if time could be controlled in a way that goes beyond how we perceive it? For instance, when I was in that car accident going over one hundred miles per hour, how was it that I was able to breakdown second by second to slow motion? Or how was it that time went missing on both of my close encounters and that time was in a flash? The relevancy of time is perhaps in dimensions we have not come to fully understand. Is it possible that strange theory of parallel universes could exist? The idea of the existence of parallelism, though possible in theory, seems very remote at best. Well, maybe it could be, but proving that would be difficult at this juncture in time. We are at our infancy in science and we will continue to grow in knowledge, if we don't wipe ourselves off this planet first.

So, if not parallel, then perhaps one life happens, then another on distant planets. I could understand the people I was meeting who had these same thoughts. I was meant to meet these people in my life. I was sure of that, but perplexed when they left me with more questions than answers. In time, understanding came that they were part of the answer for me to unravel my theory that you can have lived multiple lives, not at once. Or could you? Or are you? Perhaps that is possible and our capabilities as humans don't allow us to comprehend the reasons why. In our hearts, you look up and very few will say that we are the only life in the universe.

As a young adult, the type of young woman I wanted to meet had to be connected with this deep thinking, had to believe that we were connected in a spiritual way. This spiritualness is what I was born with and was from another life I had lived. My past was my present, and time itself was irrelevant. Tick, tock, tick, tock. In time, we will have different views on time. In 2019, a quantum physicist from the Moscow Institute of Physics and Technology conducted an experiment and reversed the flow of time. So, what will we learn and be able to do in one hundred years from now, or five hundred years from now? Yes, indeed we truly are in the infancy of human knowledge and we must be humble and kind to advance human society in science and our very existence.

I saw spirituality in a different light than most. While most saw a church, synagogue, or temple as the place of spirituality, my view would be in nature. This spirituality meant a connection to the good, not just on earth but in the universe as well. It included the belief that anything was possible, for if a UFO could make contact with a ten-year-old from Great Barrington, not just once, but twice in a two-week period, then anything was possible. I was and am connected to the universe in telepathic ways, perhaps given to me at birth and nurtured through the years. There is a memory deep within me. My recall from beyond this planet to another some say is a gift, and though it haunted me in my youth, it always kept me seeking the kind of love I felt in memory. I sought that feeling, the feeling that was deep within my soul to love and be loved. This was the feeling I was born with, to be a caring human being and love unconditionally. Well, it didn't always go so well trying to mimic a life that I had lived, but that never stopped me from trying to reach out from the depths of my soul.

Often in life, earthly humans are defined in material or social status. The hurt of meeting, then losing, those we meet because of social status is devastating in our youth. Far better to seek the true meaning of one's self than the fool's gold of precious metals. You can't take gold with you, but love knows no boundaries in both time and space. How I wish I could pass this lesson along in a world so divided and full of hate. True, we live in such a material world that the predictable first question exhaled so often is, What do you do for a living? Well, I am a seeker of truth, compassion, and love. Yes, but what university did you attend? And what do your parents do? If they only knew what my ancestors have done for this country.

These really were forget-about-it questions, and I would run off before you could say boo. Almost no one knew about those of us whose families were connected to early American history and how these generations forged America through hard work, sweat, and bravery. Let us not also forget those who we brought here against their will in the brutal act of slavery so others could advance their own personal growth at the expense of other human beings. Truth is, this went on all over the planet and was wrong then and is wrong now. Take off your blinders now. Only when we truly unite will we know the full potential of human existence.

We fought for the freedom enjoyed by Americans today and paid the price with our brothers- and fathers-in-arms. So look behind that mossy grave and see just how blind people are. Yes, we fed our neighbors with the fruits of our labors. A work day then was from sunup till sundown. You loved your friends and cherished and protected your family.

Those family roots went deep so that the family tree would be passed on, and a raconteur like myself can pass along their lives and the values so they would not be forgotten. They, too, are a part of who I am. So yes, I was passed over to go to a prestigious college for my lack of money; blind were those in admissions not to see my skills as an athlete, artist, poet, raconteur, writer, and historian. There was a pain from not counting in my early adulthood, for once upon a time in another life, I did count and was important. Now, this seeker of truth, compassion, and love is opening up to those who want to see. I see that there are other planets besides ours, I see that we must wake up and preserve our own planet earth so that we can carry on this human race.

Perhaps my prediction is as bold as those who once said that the earth was not flat. Yes, strange statement perhaps, if you set boundaries. However, the statement is unlimited if you allow the mind to ask questions and seek answers.

What was always strange for me was that I would have a vision that I was going to meet someone and sure enough, that would happen. I was never surprised, but more perplexed as to the reason. Why was I meant to meet certain people who would break my heart when I would try so hard to understand then feel diminished when I couldn't? I always questioned this idea in my mind and dreams of a former life.

Well, here on earth, working out the answers to these questions didn't really go well in my youth. I began to not want to talk about my deep feelings of spiritualness that came from my experiences of trembling as a child from the UFOs to the time I became a man. Conversations about the latest music and what was in at the time were much easier to have than conversations about a guardian angel or a UFO or communicating telepathically through space and time. Back even in the late '70s or early '80s, if you had talked about life on other planets, very few would want to even talk to you. Come on, it is still a bizarre subject, even today as more information comes out and people are more accepting to perhaps different theories of time and space and travel and life outside of ours here on earth.

In the spring of 1979, this idea was reinforced while I sat looking at the art on a gallery wall in amazement, wondering what it was about. At this point in my life, I was not an artist, but an athlete. Still, the colors and the landscape painted in a surreal fashion were amazing to me. This work intrigued me. The young woman who was there, Courtney, explained it was her boyfriend's art and that he believed he lived on another planet. Wow, that is pretty wild, I said, not really wanting to say I had those types of visions, dreams, and flashbacks all the time.

After she had left the room, I noticed a mobile hanging from her ceiling. Of course, I just could not help myself and started moving the mobile with my mind. At first, I had the mobile going in one direction and then with great concentration, had each concentric circle go in opposite directions. I thought right away of the time at Judge Keogh's house. Right as I had it going, she came back in. Oh, my God, you're moving that with your mind, she said. Well, I guess I am, I responded. Lots of explaining ensued, and the talks were about both her boyfriend's bizarre life and mine.

Through that spring, we talked a great deal about my strange life and James' life. We had an instant connection in ways that are hard to describe. I was meant to have this close connection as a validation to my understanding both mental telepathy and UFO encounters, and understanding that indeed there are other planets where life exists besides the planet earth.

One time I was with Courtney, and orbs appeared in the room. These orbs were like psychic balls of energy. There were a bit frightening because they just appeared. I was able to make them go away and know they were meant for me.

Eventually, I met James and when we met, I felt a connection to him and an understanding that there were other planets out there. The meeting was a rather unforgettable moment and I was impressed with his compassion. Courtney eventually left the local college, and they both went to their home state of Colorado, but not before opening up my views and confirming that I had very strange abilities. I was and am thankful to both of them for helping me to understand my very being in such a compassionate and caring way.

I struggled to be able to express my thoughts and beliefs for fear of ridicule and rejection. Rejection found me like an ocean wave would find the shore with a crash; it was just inevitable. Time taught me that I would find plenty of rejection, even when you're an adorable twenty-one-year-old. Rejection was only amplified by virtue of age. I thought my views on life were enough to chase any young lady away. UFOs were usually a nonstarter, as was moving objects with your mind and talk of remembering life on another planet. I remember being dumped time and time again, and one awful time I looked at my mom and said, I don't think anyone will love me, Mom. She could see my heart was broken, but assured me someone would find my kind soul.

Now out of my teens, that door to adulthood was open and the complete frontal cortex was safely formed, and by miracle after miracle I had not died. I felt at peace with my understanding of another life and another planet and the universe that surrounds us, and in doing so, sought those insights here on earth.

As I see it, a memory is implanted in your brain by experience and recalling that is like your computer bringing up a page. We bookmark a page to return and see what is on that website. Our recall to our memory is at will, but our recall in our subconscious state of dreams is different.

When we dream, we can't control everything, meaning there are both good and not so good dreams. Over time, the visions and dreams that I have had are repeated of the same locations that, as this earthly being, I have not been to; but then again, perhaps I am right that I truly did.

Yes, there is a town as clear as can be on a lake. There is a beach and the people are like humans and the surroundings are earth-like, with trees and grass and a sandy beach. The water is as fresh as a northern lake. That is all I wanted to talk about, this far away place and it's existence. Details are not what was most important; what was important is the memory about a life and place far beyond our earthly bounds.

There, people don't use words, for communication is done through mental telepathy, the same mental telepathy that sent me on that fateful night of September 1, 1969, out of the Shaw's house, running right into that UFO beam. Telepathy binds all words and language. The ultimate truth and communication are a higher standard for humans. So many people that I have interviewed on UFOs and aliens all answered the same when the subject is communication. Their answer is that mental telepathy was the form of communication used.

A movie or recall was put into me to pass on as a confirmation, not only of the existence of other planets, but through me as a life lived. I can't help that. It is who I am; I am defined by unexplainable events that were witnessed by many.

I count my blessings for those I have come in contact with on my journey of life here on this planet. I am blessed to have met my wife, Christine. I would get asked, Where did you find her? My response is, No, no, she found me there on the shores of Lake Champlain, wandering and wondering about life. She tells people, Tom is Mulder and and I am his Scully. Yeah, but you know even Scully really believed after seeing much. Here, grounded on earth, our journey was blessed with two children, Kate and Dan. How grateful and proud I am to see them grow and blossom from adorable babies to children to young adults and now adults. You look for the little things in life, moments in time, like holding your little ones on a front porch swing, walks in the woods, or kayaking on the water. We make our movies and our memories, and may they live on forever. I saw the miracle of life and birth of our children and know there is so much more. These quests and this thirst for knowledge will one day be a catalyst in science and technology for the discovery of space travel, just like the ones that visited the Berkshires and Champlain Valley that historic night of September 1, 1969. I pick the daisy to seek the answer and it changes every time.

I feel sorry for those who think the earth is flat and that our earth is the center of the universe. We are but a speck in time and our importance is found both in our existence and our ability to expand our thoughts and minds. The UFO came from somewhere to my little town here in Great Barrington, hidden in the rolling hills of the Berkshires of Massachusetts, to find me. And though I may never completely understand why, I will always know that they did!

Chapter 13

Show Me The Proof

Years had gone by and part of me wanted to just forget the part of my life with UFOs and strange abilities. Strange happenings would occur from time to time with enough infrequency for me to think that perhaps this all would pass. Then I would hear that voice, the same one I heard at the boat launch from my guardian angel. I should have known something was about to happen.

I got into my Ford van to drive from Saint-Lambert, Quebec, from my in-laws, to go to Saint-Hubert to pick up my wife, Christine, and two children, Kate and Dan. I had a funny feeling right from putting the van into drive. Saint-Lambert is on the South Shore, a suburb of Montreal. Once considered a country-like setting, that time had long passed. Now the suburbs were quite busy and this night was no different. Taschereau Boulevard was a main six-lane thoroughfare that had many intersections, and rarely did I ever not catch a red light. All these red lights were designed to keep traffic from going too fast and to keep you from acting like you were Michael Schumacher posting times for the Formula 1 Grand Prix Du Canada. There is always an idiot out there trying to beat the lights, and I was on guard as I approached one particular intersection.

I was in the far left-hand lane, and traffic came to a fast halt even though the light was green. I cautiously came to the intersection then stopped in shock. Laying in the road was a teenage girl. The car that had hit her had just sped off, leaving her to die. What the hell am I seeing? I thought. I was full of anger and fear for the lifeless body in the intersection. It caused a flashback for me and I thought of, when in my teens, I was left to die and to burn alive.

Now I would do my best to save her. In an instant, a crowd gathered and just watched. The crowd of people would not come into the boulevard to help her. Perhaps they were scared, or perhaps just in shock, but for whatever reason, no one moved except two people. The two who agreed to help me were a young man and a girl, about ten years old. To the young man I said, Do not let any car into this intersection. To the young girl I said, Listen, if a car is about to get through, yell to me. I really don't want to get hit, too.

The girl that had been hit was about sixteen years old with blonde hair. She was covered in blood as I felt for a pulse. No pulse, I yelled as I ran to my truck to get a blanket, thinking, Where the hell are the police and fire rescue? Sprinting back, I thought that if she died, at least I could cover her body and not have all those staring eyes upon her bloody body. If not, the blanket would be needed to keep her warm.

I tried to find a pulse once more before starting CPR. I was already covered with blood. In a time when you are so careful with blood I thought, no way God would give me something for helping another human being, at least not a child. This was someone's daughter, damn it, and I pictured that somewhere they were sitting at home waiting for this child to come home. I had to do my best to stop a family from experiencing complete loss and heartbreak. I thought of my wife and her dear childhood friend who had been fatally hit by a car. She did not come home. In that moment, my heart sunk and my eyes filled with tears. Oh God, not now, not tonight.

OK, here goes. Oh, crap, no pulse and no breathing. At this very moment, just as I was about to start CPR, I heard my guardian angel's voice speak to me, the same one who called to me as I was about to burn alive as a teen trapped in that car in 1976.

She said the following: Thomas, close your eyes and visualize her breathing and she will come to life. With all your heart and all your belief, do this now.

So I closed my eyes and took in a deep breath, at the same time visualizing her breathing. When I opened my eyes, she opened hers. I was absolutely shocked at what just took place and just as relieved as well. Talk about a miracle! But to me, it wasn't me at all. I was a vehicle that a miracle passed through. It took a lot of faith and belief in what I had been shown over the years, and on this night it took every ounce of faith in me.

I didn't have to preform CPR even though I was very prepared to do so. She was alive now and I could hear the screaming sirens coming in all directions. When one comes to and is in shock, you have to be concerned with so many things all at once, including tachycardia. When she came to, I calmed her down and kept her covered and still. She was speaking in French a mile a minute, and while my wife, Christine, is French and went to French schools in Montreal and Saint-Lambert, my language skills in French are next to none! The police and ambulance people spoke English and I explained what I saw. I was taken to the ambulance to be cleaned up from all the blood. The girl was load and go, and they were very fast. The ambulance attendant said my work was textbook perfect. I thought about what had happened, and how all I did was visualize and she went from no pulse or breathing to alive. Wasn't me, I thought. It was true, I was just a vehicle for energy to go through me into the the teen. Whatever that was, it brought her back to life and that's all I cared about.

The next day I called the police station to ask about the young girl. I was told she was going to make it and that the parents wanted to meet the young man who saved their daughter. I said, No, no, just tell them I am just happy that she will be OK. I was quiet about the ordeal, not wanting to say much, but at the same time thankful again to my guardian angel for letting me save a life. Yes, it had been awhile but I began to realize all this would never go away, and it was part of my journey to understand the purpose and share the lessons learned.

I should have seen the next one coming a year in advance. We were in Willsboro on Lake Champlain again in the summer. A friend asked me to help an elderly woman who was a widow and lived alone. In Buena Vista Park where we had gone for years, this is what you did. If someone needed help, then you helped. That afternoon, she asked me to stop by for a visit, as she wanted to have a talk. Not knowing what she wanted to talk about, I agreed. Her porch overlooked the wide lake and had such a pleasant breeze. She had lunch ready for me and cut the sandwich in triangles, just like Mrs. Keogh did for me all those years ago. After lunch, she began to tell me her story, but in doing so was telling me about her Mormon faith. I did not know much about the Mormon faith, even though the founder of the faith, Joseph Smith, had performed a baptism in our Alford Brook, including one to my great-great-great-grandmother, and had been in our family homestead. Today, the church would like to be called The Church of Jesus Christ of Latter-day Saints, and so I shall.

I am dying, she said to me as I finished my last bite. I want you to do me a favor, she said. At this point, I was very taken aback but agreed before even hearing another word. She continued to explain how she was dying, but did not want to burden her family, which consisted of her daughter and son-in-law and their children. However, she wanted me to talk to her daughter once she had passed. She was so sure I was going to see her and let her know how strong her faith was, and most of all, that she was at peace. We talked about her faith and how we are connected from generation to generation. Somehow, I thought all this would become clearer to me at some point. She also talked about her son who had had escaped his house that caught on fire, only to then die in a car accident years later. I had met him after the house fire, as the cabin was across the street from our cabin we rented, but I wasn't around when he died. I made my promise to her to talk with her daughter one day. With that, she gave me a hug and said her goodbye to me. I felt such an inner peace and she said a prayer and blessed me, something I cherish to this day.

Eventually I did get the news that she has passed and wondered when and if would I see her daughter. Well, I would find that answer, too, as we found a new place to rent from such a kind woman named Rosemary, whose house was a little down the lake. I met her years before at a tag sale in her yard and bought a limited edition sculpture of Texas art we named Tex! Funny how you meet people, and that's when I told her that if she ever rented, we would love to rent her house and she agreed.

The kids were thrilled at the new place we were renting. The cabin was only two cabins down from where my parents rented for nearly twenty-five years and was right on the lake. The cabin had such a charming English feel to it, so it was very fitting for us Warners, who were a tea-drinking family. From the porch you could hear the waves lapping, though the steps down to the water were quite long. The best part was they had a raft out in the water that they named Gilligan's Island. The owner's son built this impressive two-story raft that was so tall, I wasn't even tempted to jump off the top. It was a bit of a swim out there, but well worth it.

When we arrived, I heard that Kent and Barbara were at their house. Barbara was the daughter of the woman I had the conversation with who had died. All that morning I thought, How am I going to even begin to have this conversation with Barbara? Somehow I found the strength to have that conversation; after all, a promise is a promise. I was right that she never told her daughter or anyone. No one but me. The conversation was very difficult to even bring up, but somehow I managed, and I felt a sense of relief. I thought that must have been why I was sent to this spot at this time, but it turns out this was just a part of the reason I was sent to this spot and time.

I went back to our cottage for lunch and tea with my family and in-laws. Nanny and Grandpa, Christine's parents, were down on vacation with us from Saint-Lambert and we just finished lunch and tea on our porch. There were two young men out on Gilligan's Island. I wasn't paying much attention, considering their age and size. They were big lads in their early twenties and the last people I would expect to get into distress, but of course, you never know.

Suddenly, I heard just one word in a severe panicked tone: Help! With that, I raced to the door. As I was having trouble opening the door, Nanny opened the door for me. I was in such a hurry and then time went into slow motion. Running around the corner, I picked up my daughter's raft, even looking to see the warning label read that this raft was good for 180 pounds. Oh that just great, I thought, I haven't weighted 180 pounds in years! But I took it with me anyways. I flew down the flight of steep stairs and as I hit the rocky beach and entered the water, I thought how lucky I was not to have hit one single zebra mussel.

Zebra mussels are native to the Caspian Sea and found their way here to North America in ballast water from ships. They are like rabbits in water, reproducing like crazy, and before long they found a home in Lake Champlain as well. Now, one thing about zebra mussels that is painful is that they have very sharp edges. People have been known to get stitches from these and so everyone I knew started wearing beach shoes, even to swim with. These water shoes at the very least kept the bottom of your feet safe and worked pretty well on the rest of the foot as well. Too bad I didn't have any on, and it was too late now. Only later did

I find I cut my feet up pretty bad, but never felt it till much later. Funny how when you are attempting to save someone, you don't feel your own pain. I guess that is the unselfish part we choose.

There I was, three feet into the water, diving and swimming as fast as I could. I could see the two boys, both young adults, in front of me a ways out in deeper water. The one had already gone under and was about to go down for the final time as I got to him. With an uppercut under his chest, I took him out of the water and in one motion, put his arm on the raft, telling him to just hold on. It's amazing what the power of adrenaline can do.

His friend said he needed it as well and I said, Fine, just hold it and I will pull you in. I swam and pulled like crazy till I was able to stand. Then the stronger of the two boys stood and said, He took on water, he went under. Yes, I know, I said as I got him to shore and had to get the water out of his lungs. You got it, great barfing was in order and that almost made me sick myself. I have such a weak stomach for that, even with my own children! I got him up the stairs and he threw up more water before we got to my truck. The one young man was Barbara and Kent's son, and the young lad who took on the water was his best friend. After getting them into my truck, I stoped next door to their house to quickly tell them what was going on.

I ran into their house and Barbra was right there. I said to her, Call the Smith House right now and tell them I am bringing in a drowning victim. He is alert and conscious, but did take on water. Who is it? she asked. Your son's friend, I replied. This way will be faster to get him there than waiting for an ambulance.

We got to the Smith House and they took us in right away and did X-rays and all. The doctor said I did a great job getting the water out of his lungs and even a better job getting him to shore. Just the thought of it made me queasy, thinking that he was a gulp away from dying. Life truly is a fragile journey.

Now he had to take it easy and be still for a few days. After we got back, I went to the Buena Vista Park beach and when I was asked how it felt to be a hero, I just said, Nah, anyone would have done that. Yeah, Warner, they said, but you were the only one who did. As the sun started to go down, I wanted to go back and be alone as I started to shake. I had to get over what had happened and swam out to the raft, only to see my close friend Bill Sonnenstuhl had already swam there from his cottage. I was then so happy to have Bill there, as I knew he would be OK if I shed a few tears.

Right after I got up on the raft, my kind and thoughtful wife Christine swam out, carrying a bag with her. She swam out there like Katharine Hepburn on *Golden Pond*. What's in the bag, Ethel? I said. Oh, Norman, it's a few beers for you and Bill, she replied.

She passed the beers to us and swam back. Bill and I opened the beers and just as we did, a loon popped up right in front of the raft. We clinked our beers in a cheer and toast. Tommy, Bill said, God sent that loon as a sign for saving those boys

The loon went under and came back up about twenty feet away. In my mind I said thank you to the loon for giving me a sign. The loon responded back with that classic loon call and then continued swimming away. Well, Bill, I said, I think I will paint that loon. When I finished it later that winter, I named my painting "The Moon and The Loon" to remember that day, more for the message than for saving the boys. They were getting a second change at life and I another clue to my journey. I was given a Mormon Bible, called The Book of Mormon, by Kent, and the book is kept in place of honor next to our old Warner Family Bible at our homestead, here in this same house that the founder of that religion, Joseph Smith, had visited all those years ago. Guess the saying is true, what goes around comes around.

Oh, those winter months when the kids would ask if we would be going back to Lake Champlain the following summer. We were informed the cabin we just found would not be available to rent. Being a non-computer savvy person, I was challenged to find a new place. I had many choices from VRBO but as I went on one site, there was that voice again telling me to rent this one particular cabin on Willsboro Bay. I contacted the owner and reserved a time, with great family approval. Having a vacation lined up gave warm thoughts to look forward to during a deep New England winter. I kept thinking how I just wanted an uneventful vacation. The new place was perfect, sitting right on the shore facing west, and the sunsets would be fantastic. Often I would go to the end of Willsboro Point just to reflect on life as the sun would fall into the Adirondack Mountains, setting off a show of nature's beauty.

The cold, long New England winter let go according to plan and a break from the everyday work schedule was just what was needed. After arriving and unpacking what seemed to be enough to go on a journey for the entire summer, I headed back to town for a few essentials. No milk, no tea, and the Warners were known for drinking their tea. On the way back to the point, I stopped by my brother's cabin, as he and his family went to the lake at the same time.

Rosco said, Tommy, JB is looking for you. He says you're friends from way back. Rosco was right, we went back to our childhood days. I found where JB and Louise were staying and arranged a get-together at our cabin. After their arrival we went for a swim, and it was like not a day had gone by. JB and I talked about how we both survived car accidents that we should not have. He was looking for reasons why, but sometimes the answers are not always available. We just kept looking out at the water, skipping stones like we did when we were teens. Happy-go-lucky. Wow, look, five skips. I looked at him and said, JB, I think a message is going to be sent to me. I was sent to this spot for a reason. At that moment I reached into the water and picked up a rock. I was about to throw the rock when their daughter, Bridget, said, A foot, Tommy. What did you say? I asked. A foot, look at your rock, she responded. JB just looked at me, thinking I had the rock in my hand the whole time. I was stunned when I looked at the rock, as it was a grey shale color with a white imprint of a tiny foot. There on the side were initials that later would mean something important to me, but for the time being I had the rock of a tiny leprechaun foot!

Here is where this rock story got even more interesting. Prior to this, I had inherited a painting of a rather well known artist, Maynard Dixon. What we discovered in the painting was a hidden image on the painting of an alien. Even more interesting was that the painting was done in 1903. The woman who I had contacted by Internet to find how to sell the painting was a bit skeptical until I sent photos. After many times talking back and forth, I developed a friendship the woman, Gina. We even talked about our families growing up. She sent me a photo of her and her siblings when they were young. I called Gina right away and asked who one particular sister was. She responded, saying that was her sister, Debbie. She had died in a motorcycle accident. I said, September 5, 1975. Oh, my God, Tom, how would you know that? she asked. I said, I know you will find this hard to believe, but your sister was and is my guardian angel. She looked the same and was wearing the same clothes a year later when she appeared before me the night I was in my horrific car accident.

We began to talk about how I found the foot rock and the initials on the side of the rock. This alone was bizarre. I explained how I had heard a voice to reach down and pick up a rock. When I say I heard a voice, I really meant mental telepathy. Shockingly, the rock's initials were the same initials as her son's, who had died of SIDS. I sent the rock to Gina, as it was a gift sent to her through me. How much more perplexing could this get? I thought, but with my eyes I saw Gina's sister as she appeared before me a year after she died to help save me, then thought of the odds of finding her family years later. I never did sell the painting; I suppose when the time is right, the right person will come along to purchase it.

I do believe that some things are meant to happen. As much as we would love to know the reasons why at the time, we are like impatient children waiting for Christmas morning. You want the answer right now! That's not how life works and we live, we learn, and if we are receptive, we remember and understand.

The next summer, I went back to the bay to the location where I saw Debbie, my guardian angel, all those years ago. I stood there at the Willsboro boat launch and with that mental telepathy said, I have to know if you're still here. She answered, Take a picture and go home and look. Now that day the sky was a clear, blue sky. Well, I got back to our cottage and downloaded the picture I had taken and had to do a double take.

In the photo was a perfect feather cloud, even though when I looked and took the photo there were none. It reminded me of *Forest Gump* and the floating feather cloud, for the feather was a message. In the coming years, I would find a kinship to feathers. One time I went to get into my truck, and a bluebird feather was sitting on my center console. Too bad the windows were up, because that would have been easier to explain. Just how did this feather get in here? By now you would think I would be more accepting of these happenings, but the pace that they were happening now was concerning to me. Often, I would look to the night sky, thinking another visit from a UFO was imminent.

What the hell does all this mean? What was the meaning of all these clues, from saving those Latter-day Saint young men to the teen on the South Shore of Montreal, the rock, the feather cloud, and most importantly, mental telepathy? I was evolving as a human in both under-standing and acceptance of my unexplainable life. The most difficult to understand was mental telepathy. To a human being, the logic of the sub-ject just doesn't make sense. Telepathy comes from the Greek word τῆλε, tele, meaning "distant" and πάθος, pathos or -patheia, meaning "feeling, perception, passion, affliction, or experience."

Essentially, it is the transmission of information from one per-son to another without using any known human sensory channels or physical interaction. Telepathic communication is the rarest form of communication and transcends both time and space. Unless you open your mind and think outside the box, then you could never believe the subject is possible.

I went to the church of my mother, the one I was raised in, baptized in as a baby, confirmed in as a teen, and married in as an adult. No one was there, just an empty chapel. I entered the narthex the same way I had a thousand times before. A dip into the cold water. Forehead, chest, shoulder to shoulder, in the name of the Father, the Son, and the Holy Sprit. Respect was important to me. I went there not to pray, but to feel the quietness of my mind. I went there to let go of the words told to me by the priest that my UFO encounter meant I had Satan in me. To me, there were only two forces in the world, good or bad. They had nothing to do with Satan but with the choices you make as a being. I forgave that day, and with that gift of forgiveness I was able to move forward on the subject of my life. My fear of being ridiculed by others was now behind me. I could begin to talk now.

I also went to my church. I left Clyde, North Carolina, and headed to the Blue Ridge Parkway and those majestic Smoky Mountains. Knowing the Parkway was closed did not deter me. Though still closed, the Parkway was showing early signs of spring, and soon the flowering dogwood would explode, then the mountains would come alive once more. Mile by mile, I ran higher and higher, passing the warning sign for a bear sanctuary. The altitude began to climb like the spirit within me. This was beyond quiet. No cars, no people, not a sound except for the occasional passing hawk, so effortlessly drifting by above me. I screamed your name at the top of my lungs. There on this mountaintop, my echo repeated back five times. I stopped to listen to my beating heart and my very soul. Thoughts of peace overcame me that I was worthy of love and understanding. Here on this mountaintop, I found fearless inner strength that no one could take away. I would need this reminder in telling my story, for rejection of oneself cuts like a knife. Just as I rose to this mountaintop, so would the truth: it always rises to the top.

Back to Lake Champlain and my last proof gift given, as if I needed any more messages. These things you don't control; they just happen and come to me. I had just gotten back from a kayak ride with my wife. I had said, Oh no problem, Christine, the waves look just fine. Whoops. I was so wrong and we had one heck of a workout to go to Indian Bay Marina and come back. We were smart and had lunch at the marina before kayaking back. Never have we worked so much to kayak, but it was worth the effort and trip. Finally getting back, every part of my body hurt, even my buttocks. Judging by the way she got out of our kayaks, I knew Christine was sore as well, but we loved the trip anyways.

Now back, I walked the shoreline and heard that mental telepathy once again call to me to reach down into the water. If this happened a second time, how could I possibly question anything anymore? The mental telepathy said, This is a gift for you, so reach down and pick up this rock. I did, and put the rock in my pocket to look at later. Christine, our son Dan, and I sat by the shore that night, watching the sun set and the stars rise. The August air was so soothing that it was hard to leave the shore. I would wait till the next morning to even look at the rock, and a warm feeling came over me and I felt a presence of peace.

The next morning I did look at the rock I kept in my pocket. On the rock was an image of a mother holding a blond child. OK, so the child looked like me as a child. I took a picture of the rock to preserve the image and to show others, but for me this was much more. I would never ask for proof again, and the warm blanket of truth would forever encompasses my being, something no one could ever take away from me.

Chapter 14
What Do You Mean, They're Here All Ready?

I was never one who thought that perhaps that there were aliens living on earth, right before our very eyes. Of course, there are some who believe that over the years, this has become the case. I never gave this much thought at all because, well, why would I? Why would anyone? Here is how this part of the story came about. As I mentioned, I was doing research on a painting my wife and I inherited. After taking pictures of the painting with a regular camera, I downloaded the images to my computer. One of the images that opened my eyes was an image of an alien. I didn't even know back in 1903 that there was talk of the subject.

There was no doubt that having an examination of the painting done at one of the top research centers in the United States would be our first step to solve this mystery. The research center took an infrared image of the painting on both the front and back, revealing the title on the back and how the painting was done. This X-ray of the painting, along with the picture taken and the results revealed, were rather strange.

After much research, my conclusion based on years of study indicated the painting was an allegory of both Mormon and Mason nature. Oh, boy, here we go with the Mormons again! The research center listed the painting as an L. Maynard Dixon painting, or as our family referred to it, the Dixon. Dixon was very well-known at the time for allegorical paintings, but was more known for his Western paintings. After learning some of what was in the painting and not knowing what to do with the it, I thought it best at the time to leave the painting in the research center behind vaulted doors until more answers were revealed. Having the painting safe was like finding extra blankets on a twenty-below night, both necessary and comforting.

Somehow, I felt there was something special about this allegorical painting, so the search began. Here is what we found: first the number 32, then an eye of Ra symbol, the number 307, and Bainbridge. I learned that there was a correlation between the Mormon religion and Free Masonry. The founder of the Mormon church, Joseph Smith, was said to have been a member of the lodge nearby in West Stockbridge, Massachusetts and later formed a lodge in Nauvoo, Illinois. I found one of my great-grandfathers, Henry C. Warner, had written on early Mormonism. I was surprised to find that the founder of the Mormon religion was not the only Mason in West Stockbridge, as the second president of the church, Brigham Young, was as well. My great-grandpa, Henry, was a historical writer who recorded facts for generations to come. The Lester Family, who I mentioned in an earlier chapter, lived down from our homestead and they went with Joseph Smith to Nauvoo, Illinois, to follow the spiritual leader of the new faith. That was many years ago, and years later I was still hearing about them.

Back to the painting. The number 32 was the highest degree in the Scottish Rite of Freemasonry. The eye of Ra is an interesting symbol and is used by Masons and a similar eye, the all-seeing eye is on the Mormon temple. You can search that one if you like.

Interestingly enough, the artist L. Maynard Dixon was at the Bohemian Club based in San Francisco and also did paintings for the Mormon church. Every summer, the Bohemian Club, a tightly restricted and highly secretive society, would travel north for the summer gathering of these elite all-male members to Bohemian Grove, a 2,700-acre compound in the beautiful redwood groves in the Sonoma County town of Monte Rio. Their motto was Weaving Spiders, Come Not Here. It comes from Shakespeare's *A Midsummer Night's Dream*, and their meaning was that all outside concerns and business deals were to be left outside. One of the rituals, and this gets to the title of my painting, is that they had a sacrifice at an altar in front of a giant forty-foot owl. The owl sacrifice is to the god Moloch. Not that I personally believe they ever sacrificed anyone at the altar (let's hope not anyway), but it was a ritual just the same. Moloch was the chief god of the Ammonites, who were from Ammon in Eastern Canaan, and in 307 BC, two hundred boys were sacrificed and burned to Moloch.

There are pictures online about the Bohemian Grove owl and ritual, none that I care to share. This was the 307 in the title of my painting. If you don't think that owl is in our everyday life, open up your wallet and look at the United States dollar bill. Just to the left of the number on the back is the tucked in owl.

Onto the last word in the title: Bainbridge. Of course, I thought it was an address until I was able to think outside the box, and that brought me right back to the Mormons and the founder, Joseph Smith. I discovered the Bainbridge Trial, also known as The People vs. Joseph Smith the Glass Looker. It was said that Smith had strange abilities that were challenged in court. I had another hint at this unusual painting.

The painting itself is of six apples on a hill. Of course, the Mormon faith started on a hill and had six original members. Six is also used in a sign for directions. There are six directions in the universe to go: up, down, east, west, north, or south. Apples also stood for the fruit of knowledge, but what knowledge was the artist referring to? There were hidden symbols in the painting that I would describe as hieroglyphics.

There were also twelve leaves in the painting in a distinctive pattern of five leaves, three leaves, then four leaves. The numbers five, three, and four are the ratio of integers that form a right angle. Say what you will, but in the Mormon religion, you raise your right hand up to form a right angle. Yes, five, three and four! I just felt a closeness and curiosity to what they were trying to say.

Here is where all this about my painting got weird, and for me to say weird is a great understatement! North of Great Barrington at the time was a research center named after former congressman Silvio O. Conte. The place was perfect to immerse oneself in genealogical research and when I was there before, the place was packed. I just woke up one morning and heard a mental telepathy voice say to go there, and so I was off. On this return trip, I expected it to be just as busy, even though I had heard that the place was going to be closing. Upon arriving to a near-empty parking lot, I was hesitant to enter the building.

In the entryway was the Congressman's roped off desk, where he worked tirelessly for his district and constituents. He was very well-liked and always sent back to Washington to represent the district. I stood there looking at his desk, and much to my surprise, an alarm went off. How could I set off an alarm by looking at it? I was thinking, Oh, crap, I just set off an alarm and never did anything but look at it. How the heck did I do that?

Of course, I waited till someone came out to tell me what happened. In a rather accusatory tone, I heard a voice call out to me, You must have touched something. I responded, Well actually, no, I did not. But thanks for turning off the alarm. He looked at me with a strange expression, like he had seen a ghost. He stated he was the only person working there and for me to come to his desk if I needed any help. He said it was just me and another man there.

I looked over at the man and right away got a weird feeling. Then I realized he was talking to me by mental telepathy. He got up and walked over to me. I need to look for someone, I said. Stand back, he said. He went onto my laptop and his hands typed faster than was humanly possible. Now, tell me when you're done, he said as he walked away. When I was finished, he came back and and did the reverse. I was dumbfounded that he did what he did. He then asked why I was interested in Masonic Knights Templar. Wait, I thought, I never said anything about the Masonic Knights Templar. This confirmed to me that not only was he communicating telepathically, but also reading the thoughts I was trying to keep private.

Before long, we were talking about my painting and how there were symbols in the painting, along with the depiction of an alien. He asked if the painting was in a safe area and I assured him that it was, and even told him where. I was so confident that it was safe and felt safe telling him about the painting. It is safe behind vaulted doors. I can say with certainty that it is safe, I told him. As I looked at him, something was different; it took me a few minutes to realize what. I was trying not to stare, but then it hit me. Oh, my God, he doesn't blink. He seemed to catch on, too, that I was curious about him now, and he went back to his corner.

A few minutes later, the gentleman who was the employee called me to his desk and asked where the other man went. What do you mean, where did he go? I asked. The only way out is past me, and I didn't see him go. Stay here while I look around, the employee said. Sure enough, when he got back he looked so disturbed and said that he was nowhere in the building. At this point, I was a bit freaked out and said I had to leave. I drove back to Great Barrington, wondering the whole time what had just happened. Why was he so interested in me and my painting?

When I got home, there was a note left in my notebook and I had no idea what the meaning was. The note said, "IN GUG WE TRUST." I called the center right away and the gentleman answered. I asked, Did you leave a note in my notebook? No, I didn't. It must have been that guy you were talking to, he responded. I told him what was written and he said he had no idea what it meant. Well, that made two of us. I had a very strange feeling about this. Not long after, the center was closed for good and it would be a number of years before the expression "IN GUG WE TRUST" would come up again. I would have to wait, but did not have to wait long to take my painting back. Sadly, when I got my painting back, the image of the alien was gone, as were the symbols. I was told that my painting was still valuable and that the woman's father who worked there was a 32nd Degree Knights Templar. I knew the fight over the image would be a lost cause, even though I still had pictures with the alien image. All the same, I could not understand how a painting from 1903 would contain the image of an alien. What was in the painting that they had to take out? Was it the symbols or the drawing of the alien? As strange at this sounds, and as strange as the encounter was, I believe with all my heart that the strange man from the center was a human-alien hybrid. This may have been my first encounter while fully awake and aware, but it would not be my last. Humans involuntarily blink about fifteen times per minute. As humans we have to blink, but human-alien hybrids do not.

On a cold winter day a few yeas ago, I was at the Bay Y, a local shopping market in Great Barrington, and was just going in for a few things before going to pick up my wife from her work at Mason Library. Since I was running a bit late, I felt lucky my list was short. Off with the cart I went, and in the first aisle I noticed a woman who appeared to know me by how long she looked at me.

Now, I am not the best at remembering names, and I continued on shopping thinking, Do I know that woman? Two aisles later I saw her again, and then again in the last aisle I was in. I felt a familiar yet strange feeling as I made eye contact again. Dang, she is reading my mind. But who is she? I thought. Where do I know her from, and why is she following me? Now I was done with my shopping list and headed for the checkout counter. With a quick glance to pick up Dan's Reese's Peanut

Butter Cup, I was shocked to see her now in front of me in the line. She had nothing to check out and grabbed a candy bar. You're the artist, she said. Now at this point, I was so pleased to be recognized as an artist, yet perplexed, wondering who she was. No doubt she knew who I was.

I reached into my wallet to hand her my art business card when I had the time to look into those strange eyes staring back at me. Here we go again. She was not blinking. She said, I know who you are and where you live. You are safe. I am looking out for you. With that she left, just buying that one candy bar and paying with cash. I got out of the store as fast as possible and looked around for her, but did not see where she had gone.

When I got to my wife's workplace, Christine looked at me and said, How did you get that burn in your jacket? Now don't ask me how, but in that short time in that store, a burn was put in to my fluffy, furry jacket. What the hell? How the hell? I thought. I felt nothing and never remembered seeing anyone that close to me. Perhaps I should have been concerned, but overall I wasn't. Besides, the woman did say she was there looking out for me.

So when people say aliens are here, are there different types of aliens? Well, perhaps there are; but who can say for sure? I only can speak to my personal experiences and then the experiences of people I meet. Once, I had conversation with someone I will call Z. I would never reveal someone's name if I knew they did not want to be or could not be known. Z worked in a special job in a special place.

This job was so special that in doing it, Z saw things that he did not really want to see. Z had the talent of reading lips at a great distance. This was an amazing skill! I was told he knew a lot about UFOs and aliens, so I was very anxious to talk to him. When we talked, I told the story of the time at the research center and my note saying "IN GUG WE TRUST." There was an eerie silence till Z's voice cracked nervously as he said, I will send you a message. When I received the message, there was a drawing of what he had seen: a very tall alien and two men, one saying to the others, In GUG we trust until his salvation. Z wrote, "Whoever gave you that knows way to [sic] much." I never got to ask more questions and that was the last conversation I had with Z, for both of our protection.

The next time I heard of that expression, I was given a hint that the expression it was based on was some sort of Egyptian meaning or myth. Perhaps I will know more over time. This all made me think of the Dixon painting, which also had alien and mystic meanings, and perhaps there were answers in that painting and someone did not want the deep secrets revealed. I know I met two human-alien hybrids of such high intelligence and psychic skills. I wondered, Where did they go, and where are they now? I know they know where I am and though that should, and does, concern me at this point in my life, it does so mildly. This all just made me think that not only are there aliens here, but that they have been here for a very long time.

Chapter 15

There Were Others

The growing interest in my experiences was quickly becoming apparent to me, and having the entire story told was my only goal. The phone rang, and not recognizing the number on the caller ID I hesitated, but answered anyway. Hello, is this Tom Warner? said a voice.

Depends, I said.

Is this the Tom Warner who had a close encounter with a UFO?

Now that really depends, I answered suspiciously. Who am I speaking with?

I'm Adam Reilly, WBGH, Boston. If you're the Tom Warner who had a close encounter, I would like to interview you.

Yes, it is me, and yes, you can interview me, as long as you do this in an honest format. When would you like to do this?

We will be out to Great Barrington tomorrow, Adam said.

Great, I answered. I will see you tomorrow.

I started thinking how all this was coming forward. I began to think about all those people who talked to me about UFOs, and the strange happenings in my life, and how their lives affected me in so many ways.

The expression of letting the cat out of the bag came to my mind, but I had already done a number of interviews, both locally and internationally, and a rather long interview in a documentary done by Maldonado Productions. He had called me and said he was doing a senior college thesis for a film studies program at Harvard. The interview was well done and I enjoyed seeing his finished work on the Internet. In time, the documentary was taken down and in asking Google about it, I was told access to that file was forbidden. What the hell does that mean? Oh, that didn't sound good. Forbidden!

Actually, I never thought I would be talking about the subject of UFOs and I was just fine with never saying any more; but over time, more and more people came forward, and I reluctantly came to the conclusion to come forward as well.

There, in my inbox, was a message asking me about one of my paintings on my art website, www.tomwarnerwatercolors.com, called *Forgotten Spirt*. The story of the painting is that my family has lived in the same house since 1835, and over the years, many stories have been told of its history. One that was handed down was that in the 1830s, Indian chiefs used to stay with us on our property so that they could visit fallen warriors who had been killed in the battle with General Talcot at Great Barrington, Massachusetts. I was never told where exactly this site was, but I have a pretty good idea. *Forgotten Spirit* is the painting of a Native Spirit some have heard and others have seen. She is on a path we now call Spirit Path, and the flowers represent the rebirth of her spirit. Notice the face in the tree watching over the path and the spirit. Now Forgotten Spirit will always be remembered!

With all that being said, I was asked would I please walk a property and tell the woman what I felt. Her mom had died, and since I knew who the family was, I agreed to do so. Little did I know at the time, but this was the same area that a UFO was spotted on the same night as my first encounter. I had known the woman, Debbie, from my high school in Great Barrington, and she was to meet me there. Upon arriving, no one was there, and it was getting late, so I went to the edge of the woods behind their property. I felt a pulling action, asking me to come deep into the woods. Though warmly dressed in a hoodie, the goosebumps were overwhelming. When Debbie arrived, I told her what I felt and then she asked if I would walk through the now-empty house. Though empty, I could see what was there in my vision. At this point, I thought, I don't want to do this anymore. I brought up how this strange ability I sometimes had went back to when I was a child and had my UFO encounters. I told her about them and the time they happened. The look on her face was alarming. You need to talk to my close friend, Thom Reed. He had one at the same time as you, and he knows of your case. Not sure how she knew that, or how he knew about my case, but I let that go and was more than willing to chat with him. I heard there were others who saw it that night, so I wasn't overly surprised to hear Reed had as well.

Now I knew who Thom was from high school, but we never hung out at all. I can only remember seeing him a few times, perhaps at a bonfire or just passing in the halls of Monument Mountain, and never heard of his encounter while back in high school. Debbie placed the call and introduced him to me by phone.

The thing that most impressed me about Thom was his determination to try and understand what happened on that September 1, 1969, night. I helped in researching and retracing where he had been that night. After all, I still live here in the Berkshires. It was very interesting finding the places he went that night before heading home with his mother, brother, and grandmother. Old timers told me about the hamburger joint they ate at. Researching at the local library, I confirmed Butternut Basin as the location of his story and that indeed they had a horse show earlier that day. However, there was nothing in any local papers about what had happened to us that night, contrary to what some claim. It turns out the local paper just did not want to write about a UFO story back in 1969. People back then were reluctant to talk, so I understand their thinking.

Thom's father, Howard Reed, had pushed to find the truth, and according to Thom, he died under very unusual circumstances that would make anyone question just what had happened. Honoring his dad by helping Thom to understand this all was a good enough reason for me to come forward. I knew there were others from hearing chitchat on the subject from time to time. I only wanted to come forward if the story was going to be told in an honest way, not just about one person. I wanted coming forward to be voice of healing for all involved on that fateful night and others who had similar experiences.

As an artist, I wanted to do a painting of that night based on both our stories, and interviewed Thom for months on the subject, asking detailed questions so that I could get the feel for the painting I was about to do. In doing so, I got to know his story in detail. Though the painting was about both our experiences, I put Thom as the face of the child because he was so forward with telling his story; I was not convinced that I would be so open but eventually, I would agree to tell mine as well.

In showing the painting to a woman in nearby South Egremont, Massachusetts, she asked to speak to me outside. You have had close encounters, she said. Why do you say that? I asked. Because, no one could paint fear and terror like you did without experiencing that, she responded. I admitted to her that I had indeed had close encounters and told her my story, and how it happened the same night and time as a number of friends.

I went on to talk about the orbs in the painting and how I had experienced them as they appeared in a room. I said, They were balls of psychic energy, sent by aliens. The woman began to cry, saying her own daughter had that happen, too, and that she could see an alien in the room. She gave me a hug and thanked me for helping her understand the subject and to believe her daughter. She had a lot of healing to do, and I can only pray they are both now doing well.

The painting is called *UFO Boy*, and is now part of the famous Roswell International UFO Museum in Roswell, New Mexico. After I donated the painting to the Roswell International UFO Museum, they sent a certificate and awarded me a lifetime membership to the museum. I have yet to visit and yet to be invited as a guest speaker. So check it out and ask to see the painting while you are there.

Not long after the painting was put into the museum, I received a call from the Roswell Daily Record and spoke with Jerry Heck, who was a staff reporter. One thing would lead to another, and the another was a radio interview.

Thom gave me a heads up that they would be calling me, and I was fine with that. I thought doing the radio interview would get the entire story out there, not just what happened to Thom. After all, it wasn't just Thom and I that this happened to, but up until now the media was fixed on Thom like a missile on a target. I, on the other hand, wanted the entire story told or I would just back off completely.

So the phone rang and it was Dr. J. Andy Ilias from Los Angeles. Dr. J, as he is known, is a UFO radio talk show host whose program is on Coast to Coast. Well, actually, it is world-wide broadcast with a very large listening audience. I was told over eight million. Well, that's a lot! The program was going to have Thom, the Roswell Daily News reporter, me, and Cheri Canup Allfrey.

Cheri worked for United Space Alliance, which was a primary contractor for NASA. When the space shuttle was coming in, they could see something following it. The only problem was that a no-fly zone was enforced in that area, and so nothing should have been there. The interview was very interesting and though I was told every one of Dr. J's programs were recored, this one somehow disappeared. I was seeing a pattern of my UFO information disappearing, and it was becoming concerning to me. How can I get my story out there if everything keeps disappearing?

As I was doing my part of the interview from the Warner Homestead library, I received a message via Facebook. It was from my childhood Lake Champlain friend, Judi Clarke-Fowler, saying, Holy crap, I'm listening to you from Gaeta, Italy, and we have to talk! I typed back, Yes, right after this interview!

Then I read her words: Awesome interview, however we need to talk! My brother, sisters, and mom witnessed a UFO at our camp! They sent two guys from Plattsburgh Air Force base the very next day! This thing was hovering right over us…we yelled, Mom! And she came flying out and told us to go inside, but we were so mesmerized by the colors and then it shot like hell right across the lake over to Vermont! I'm talking… whoosh!!! Gone, in a split damn second! That is one second per mile. Talk about getting around fast.

Turns out their UFO sighting was on the same night of September 1, 1969. Judi continued telling me how when the Air Force came down, they split up the children and told them to do drawings of what they saw. I was amazed to hear her description of the UFO and remembered the multicolor lights and how they were so fixed on the craft. She said, I remember how my brother Bill went right under it. Bill said he remembers the bright lights. They were bright all right, some of the brightest lights I had ever seen.

We talked for hours on the subject and how much fun we had as kids growing up in those summer months on beautiful Lake Champlain. Willsboro was a great summer vacation place, and as much time as we all spent together we didn't talk to each other about our experiences. We all would lay on the sandy beach that had a little sandy hill down to the water's edge. We were looking up, searching to see any shooting stars, but truth was we were looking for more; yet we never said a word about our close encounters.

Judi, nor her sister or brother, Bill Clarke, talked about that night. But now I had come forward, and one by one they would. Judi had moved back stateside and I was looking forward to seeing her after so many years. We arranged a meeting, but sadly just one week before we were to get together and record an interview, she died of a brain aneurysm. I felt so crushed by the news of her passing. Her voice echoes in my mind talking abut the subject. Her brother Bill picked up the UFO baton to tell their family's story, for which I am very grateful and so very proud of my friend, Bill.

Not long after the interview on Coast to Coast, more people came forward. I spoke with my childhood friend, Joanne Thompson, on the subject. I told Joanne about how I had her initials on my ceiling as a lad just so I could smile and get to sleep, because back then I was so scared to sleep, so afraid that the UFOs would come back again. We were kids in grade school and hearing her laugh now was just like turning back the clock to the fifth grade. I still had my teddy bear from then and was happy to still have Joanne as my friend. I met up with Joanne at her Berkshire home, an amazing, neat old place called the Chestnut Lodge. The late October air was as crisp as the Berkshire foliage and I could smell the distinctive burning of apple wood in her fireplace.

The Chestnut was once a sea captain's home; it was even a stagecoach stop in the Berkshires. I expected to see the ole sea captain in this mysterious setting. As I entered the Lodge, I felt like I drifted back in time to the early 1800s, with the fieldstone fireplace alive with a crackle and glow. We talked about both our stories and my nerves were on edge the entire time, thinking I had to drive back to Great Barrington and hoping I would not have another close encounter.

Joanne jokes that it was because of my connection to her as kids that the UFO appeared to her and her mother, and perhaps she was right. They were driving on Route 41 heading towards Great Barrington. She says the following: We could almost see it from Division Street, quite a distance from the center of town. It was flat along the railroad tracks and river area. It was very low to the ground, panning back and forth, searching for something or someone. At first we thought that it might be a helicopter. There, as the road rises up steeply, at one point we were above it in altitude. I told Mom to pull over and shut off the car. If it was a helicopter, shouldn't we be hearing it?

We rolled down the windows and heard nothing, and saw what looked like panels. Mom said we should get out of our car, but I said no. Then, silently it rose up, almost even with us and I saw panels and lights all over. We could have hit it with a rock. It hovered for about three to five minutes, taking off straight over us, over the mountain towards Lake Mansfield, the same place my cousin saw it.

When she told me that it happened on November 1979, I realized that I was at Lake Mansfield that night, reflecting on the direction of my life. At the same time this was going on with Joanne, her sister was driving home in front of them. I spoke with her sister and she, too, had experiences and lost time, and she also said the UFO headed towards Lake Mansfield. This was the same beach where her cousins had a close encounter the very same night of September 1, 1969.

The one person I remembered that Labor Day night, just as clear as can be, was Melanie. I saw her there, crouched right in a corner, with her eyes crying out for help. It was one of the most frightening looks I had ever seen. I did not see that face again until I started high school. I was a freshman at Monument Mountain and I was hurrying to get to class when I opened a door and there she was, the girl from the UFO. Oh, my God, to this day, just thinking of the look in her eyes brings me chills. I had to find who she was. I turned around to follow her and learned her name was Melanie. A year later, I learned she had brother and sister. For years, I tried to contact her brother to talk. At the time, he lived on Cape Cod, Massachusetts, and I called with no response. I was told he was contacted by Thom Reed, who had contacted Joanne as well.

Thom was looking for some of the witnesses to his close encounters, but the ones I was hearing about were up in Great Barrington, not down where he had his close encounter, at the Old Sheffield Covered Bridge. We were, however, a confirmation for each other to the facts that happened that night.

Eventually, I did get to talk to Melanie's brother and he told me his story. He said how how he and his two sisters and mother and father were up at Lake Mansfield, just over a mile from my house, having ice cream cones when the UFO appeared over the lake. Just when I thought he would open up on the subject, he clamed up and ignored my calls, and I thought that part of the story would not get told.

By chance, Melanie was helping a friend and was outside our local grocery store. I had not seen her since my high school days, but recognized her with just a glance into her eyes; they were the same caring eyes that looked upon me in the UFO. We exchanged a hug and hello greeting and said we would chat sometime. I was in such a hurry, but knew right at that moment we had to talk. Though it took me some time to get the nerve to call her, I finally did. You could hear a pin drop the day I told Melanie how I remember her on that UFO. Luckily for me, Melanie did not clam up. She was so brave in coming forward and even did hypnosis to understand what had happened that night. Not all can be so brave as her, and I don't put anyone down for not coming forward. Melanie remembered the colored lights and parts on the UFO. The part of her story that was so frightening was that she woke up alone on the Lake Mansfield beach the very next morning, not having any idea how she got there, and then had to walk home.

Another person who came forward was a former neighbor, Jane Green, who lived a street away from us. She lived with her husband and children and back in 1969, they owned the popular Harper's Drug Store in Great Barrington. The Greens were a very well-respected family back then. Her two boys were closer to my older brothers' age and her daughter, Toby, was closer to mine. All those years went by before I would hear her story. There was so much silence through the years. I feel blessed that I got the opportunity to sit down and talk to this wonderful woman about her connection to this historic night in the Berkshires. Right about after sunset, Jane was on her way back to Great Barrington from Stockbridge on Route 7, along with her friend Mary DeGrace. She noticed lights up in front of them and slowed down, thinking there was an accident. Slowly as they approached, they discovered this was no accident in front of them. Jane told me how the craft was only about fifteen feet off the ground. She, like many others, described seeing strange colored lights, colors she had never seen before. This craft was so close to the side of the road, and it sat there for a few minutes before slowly rising and then rapidly departing the area and going over Monument Mountain near the high school.

All the way to Great Barrington, Jane said nothing to Mary and Mary said nothing to Jane. After talking to her husband, Bernie, they went to see Tom J. at the local radio station, WSBS. They did not get the response they thought they would get after seeing such a surreal event. When they got to the station, Tom was calm and just started to laugh, saying, You must have smelled swamp gas. Jane said to me, I was mad as hell at him. Swamp gas, ha! I knew what I saw.

Back in 1966, the Air Force tried out their hypothesis that swamp gas caused UFO sightings in Hillsdale, Michigan. The Hillsdale Country issued a twenty-four page report challenging the swamp gas theory. Once word got out about the term swamp gas, it was easy to try to discredit those witnesses who were just trying to say what they saw.

In the short time Jane was at WSBS, others called, telling similar stories. By the next day he, too, was convinced, as a number of people reported the event all over the South Berkshire towns of Great Barrington and Sheffield. He opened his newscast the next day with the report that people had seen a UFO over the South Berkshires!

As word was getting out about my story, another friend and former schoolmate, Lori Potter, contacted me. Her story was tied to me as well, though she nor I knew that until we talked. Lori and I were in school together, from grade school right through high school. When Lori told me her story, I thought, Oh, wow, here we go again on a connection to UFOs. I have to go back to where Lori was and where I was the night she saw her UFO up close.

The year was 1984 and I was a long ways from the Berkshires, and as I looked out from Hurricane Ridge in the Smoky Mountains, I had a sudden feeling I had to come back home. It was the same telepathy as I had all those years before on September 1, 1969. I was being called home and I knew it. That night, I packed up my small amount of belongings, left a note at my work, and took off. I called my mom, saying, Look, I will be home by Father's Day, but don't tell Dad, I want this to be a surprise. Off I went on my slow journey north driving up on the Blue Ridge Parkway till eventually on a Saturday night, my '77 Ford F-100 broke down in Pennsylvania.

I was so upset and told the man I was just trying to make it home for Father's Day. No problem, it's just a water pump, he said. I'll get you on your way. With the help of one of his friends, Jake had me on my way in no time. Although I was tired, I continued on and was relieved to see the Welcome to New York State sign. Now just a ride up the Taconic State Parkway and I would be on the Berkshire's doorstep. Getting off the Taconic, I pulled into the town of Hillsdale, just eight miles from my home.

Suddenly I felt woozy and pulled over into the Four Brother's Pizza parking lot. Being late at night and after so many miles of driving, I thought I would rest my eyes and then drive home. I was always so good at a fifteen minute nap and rarely would they go any longer. How can that be as when I came to, nearly four hours had passed? I drove the rest of the way with a very perplexed feeling but sort of shrugged it off, until years later when I heard Lori's story of the same night and time and area.

She said, Tom, yes, it was around 12:30 at night. My ex-husband, Ron, and I had been at a friend's house watching movies. So Ron and I were going home on this dirt road in Sheffield. We had driven this road many times before at night. In the sky I noticed two very bright lights hovering above our car. At first we thought it was a helicopter. After a few minutes, we got curious because the lights continued to hover over us. When we turned right onto Route 41 in Sheffield, the lights got behind us and actually followed us. Ron had noticed that the clouds, stars, and moon disappeared at the time. This scared us both and I felt like I was paralyzed, then suddenly the lights disappeared. The following evening, my sister-in-law woke us up at 3 AM and showed us how she was watching the lights over the mountain. It was so spooky. Our electronics in our house went crazy and our poor dog ran upstairs to hide.

If something happened to me that night, I would not be able to tell you. All I know is that when I was in that area, another UFO was as well.

Even as I write this, people are coming forward. Two schoolmates who rode the same bus in high school with me, whom I have the utmost respect for, Sue and Shayne, let me know they too had seen a UFO in our neighborhood. More strange reports of UFOs in the Great Barrington area have been reported. According to the National UFO reporting center, two cases were from April of 2017 and April of 2018, just a half mile from my home; so the story continues. Yes, spooky and for sure there were others.

July 1, 2020, Netflix released *Unsolved Mysteries*, and "Berkshires UFO" told the story of September 1, 1969. I was told this would go out to many people and by the next day, I was getting calls. I didn't know really what to expect, and was so happy that so many people said they were thrilled that I and the others came forward to tell our story and that it was helping others. Yes, helping others was the only reason I came forward to do interviews on radio, print, television, and now here, to open my soul in my autobiography. *Unsolved Mysteries* brought attention to this subject and the door to conversation is now wide open. No turning back now, just going forward with the truth.

After the show aired, we took a week vacation up to Lake Champlain, and one of the first calls I got was from a Mike Sisino. Mike began the conversation by telling me that he was a thirty-year veteran of the Vermont State Police, and he had my attention right away; I wanted to hear what he had to say. He told me how his wife watched the show and at breakfast the next day she insisted, Hey, you have to watch this show tonight. So that night on Netflix, they went to watch episode five, "Berkshires UFO." When the show came to the part where I was in my studio showing my painting of the UFO, Mike sat up in his chair and said, That's it, that is what I saw.

On September 1, 1969, the sun had already set and Mike Sisino was driving home in a faded red wooly jeep with his mom. They lived close to the water on Beach Plum Lane in their hometown of Nissequogue, New York, on the north shore of Long Island. Out of nowhere, the UFO was over them and continued heading over the sound on a direct course towards the Berkshires of Massachusetts. Mike's dad was chief of police of Nissequogue, and when he got home, Mike and his mother told his dad what they had seen. His dad confirmed there were calls coming in with the exact description. I was very grateful for Mike reaching out to me after seeing "Berkshires UFO" as a confirmation to that historic UFO night and also all the others who have come forward too. Thank you. Thank you so much for your bravery in telling the truth.

Chapter 16

Where Do We Go From Here?

In my forward, I said I would give my message that really has been weaved throughout this book. My ultimate conclusion on this matter was formed not only by my own personal experiences, but also those of others. When you see something with your own eyes, like I did with the UFO on September 1, 1969, you look for answers as to what your eyes are taking in, and I wondered why this UFO was there for me.

Here, after more than fifty years have passed, I got a message from a friend, Rick Castello, who had set up his incredible telescope up on Baldwin Hill in the South Berkshires. My son, Dan, and I went up to have a view on a crisp, clear night. There, with the help of Rick's telescope, our eyes saw Jupiter and the wonderful moons Io, Callisto, and Europa. Then we moved on to Saturn and the rings. But then we went deep into space. As Rick began to talk about all the stars and planets out there, something occurred to me. The numbers out there tell me I was right.

If there are a billion stars per galaxy and there are ten billion galaxies that means there are a billion trillion stars. If there are a billion trillion stars, then how many planets contain life, even life similar to ours here on planet earth?

Do I think there are other life forms out there? Of course I do. Once upon a time, humans thought the earth was flat and low and behold, our earth is a sphere. So a simple fact we know today was once thought to be ridiculous. Someday in human history, we will know of other planets with life forms just like ours. I know they exist and many people have come to the same conclusion as myself. They visited this earth, telepathically communicated to me, abducted me, and left me with more questions than answers on that historic day in 1969. We tag sharks, they tag humans. I'm OK with that being sort of scientific data, and if that betters humankind, then I will live with that.

Truth, you see is like cream; eventually it rises to the top, and sooner or later the truth about UFOs and the existence of life forms beyond ours will become known. The one theme that was consistent over all these years is that the truth on the subject of UFOs has been covered up. It is not breaking news by any means that our government would cover up anything. Ever look up Project Blue Book? Well, that only scratches the surface of the truth. Just enough to say that they are looking, while newspapers articles written make those who saw these odd occurrences out to be just plain nutters or people smelling swamp gas. Even the expert, J. Allen Hyneck, started out as a skeptic, but slowly changed his views after time and cases studied. Swamp gas, give me break!

Back when Richard Nixon was president, he was close friends with comedian Jackie Gleason, who was a Nixon supporter and golfing buddy. I can only imagine how much fun that must have been with Jackie, who was one of the most hilarious comedians of the time! Jackie was also very interested in UFOs. So one night, Nixon picked up Jackie and drove him to a government location. The shocked guard, seeing it was President Nixon, let him through. When inside the location, he was shown aliens. I would have loved to have seen Jackie's expression on that one! Needless to say, when the story got out via his second wife, Jackie was not happy. People did not want to come forward then, but slowly more and more would over time. Nixon was not the first nor would be the last to have encounters or talk about UFOs.

In 1969, future president and then governor, Jimmy Carter, who was about to give a speech, witnessed a UFO. When running for president, he was asked on the campaign trail if he would finally tell the truth to the American people about UFOs. Without hesitation, he said yes, he would. Well, as we all know he was elected president in 1976 and as promised, he went on to declassify what the CIA knew on the subject. The CIA turned down his request, and when he asked director and future president George H. W. Bush, Can you tell me what the CIA knows about UFOs? Bush said to Carter, Mr. President, you have no need to know. Why would the president of the United States have no need to know? Isn't he the commander in chief? Let that sink in for a while.

Later that year, Carter backed off the subject, saying that the release of such documents would cause national security defense implications. Oh, really, do tell. This all was more confirmation that there was more out there. At what point in our history will we talk about UFOs openly for the betterment of mankind? I think the American public can handle the truth, but apparently the government does not feel the same, at least not up to this point! For now, we are better to look to the scientists for information and those first hand witnesses who are willing to talk.

We know that scientists are looking for answers in all fields of this subject. Even back in 1959, ten years before a UFO would make an appearance over the Berkshires, physicists Giuseppe Cocconi and Philip Morrison wrote an article called "Searching for Interstellar Communications" in the British journal *Nature*, said to be one of the most scientific journals on this planet. These guys were experts in their field, and Morrison worked on the Manhattan Project and later quantum physics, nuclear physics, and high-energy astrophysics. So science was looking, even back then, which is why the Drake equation came about, to search the probability and estimate the number of extraterrestrial civilizations in our Milky Way galaxy.

I first heard of the Drake equation in a documentary by Maldonado Productions that I was also the subject of. Astronomy professor Grant Wilson, at the University of Massachusetts, went on in this documentary to explain the Drake equation. To me, it is more of an opening of the mind, for when we ask questions we begin to search for answers. Science was and still is looking for those answers. Human existence never sits still, yet we must advance in ways that do not endanger our planet, the way we are now on our current path. We need to all wake up. How many warnings do scientists have to give?

Today, NASA even has a planet-hunting telescope called TESS, short for Transiting Exoplanet Survey Satellite. Low and behold, they found an earth-size planet. In the next two years, they estimate that TESS will find three hundred more planets. So much is out there that we just do not understand, but if we don't search and seek answers, we will never find them. For me, this is all just more proof of the existence of life that has visited us before and will continue to visit in the future. I like to think of UFOs as scientists and explorers from distant galaxies and other planets. They are just searching for answers, too. For us humans, we have such a long time to go to even start to catch up to what's out there. A witness said it took the UFO one second to cross Lake Champlain, which is close to six miles. That calculates to a little over 21,000 mph. That's 6 miles a second, 360 miles a minute, and over 21,000 miles per hour. That kind of shoots down the theory that these UFOs are man-made.

I was almost done taking about the subject of UFOs and aliens, both human-hybrids and other versions, and then in May 2018, Boston TV WGBH's Adam Reilly called me for an interview. Though I knew the interview was a short news segment, I wanted to clarify the event as best I could. Yes, the story was condensed, but the points were well-given as to the overall story of the UFO visiting the South Berkshires.

Adam had done a very fine job, but in a short time I would find parts of the interview he had produced for WGBH were being used by UFO media to tell the story their way. My fear was the UFO media, in doing so, was burying the truth rather than telling the truth. They were saying this was a Sheffield, Massachusetts, incident and others were just a witness to that incident, and that none of us had been close to what happened in Sheffield. That was just not true at all! After hearing this on the web, I was so concerned that the truth could be manipulated that I was ready to give up on the subject. As fate would have it, a phone call changed my mind.

That day, my daughter, Katie, had stopped by our house for lunch and listened to the incoming call message from the folks at *Unsolved Mysteries*. Kate loved the show when it last aired. At first, I was hesitant to return the call, but with Katie's encouragement I went ahead anyway, and I am glad I did.

The idea was to tell the story of the September 1, 1969, UFO over the South Berkshires, and they wanted to talk me. Over time, I agreed to tell the story because I was convinced they would tell the real story of that night in a honest way. I had and have the utmost respect for their company and every worker on their staff, from the front office to the field workers and director. Though I knew that telling the story meant I would be opening myself up to ridicule, and there was plenty all ready going around here in the South Berkshires of Massachusetts. I thought it was time the complete and real story of that September 1, 1969, night came out. I was willing to wait on my autobiography. I felt the need to tell the complete story of my life on this subject and from that day, I wanted to say how there was more than just that September night.

Everyone who had a close encounter was equally important in that story. I was not a witness, but a confirmation that all of us had our own personal experiences, equally important to the overall story.

Fifty years have passed since the September 1, 1969, incident and my experiences on that night. There was buzz about UFOs in the south Berkshires and chitchat had increased on a weekly basis. I overheard two strangers talking about that 1969 event, and after a while one asked me if I had heard of the UFO story. There is an old New England expression: Was ya there, Charlie? Ay, yup, I was there all right. I had really considered just keeping quiet, but I felt the real story of that historic night would not be told until I opened up. This was about the entire community and those affected, and I hope in writing this book, more will come forward and change the perception of UFOs and those who encounter them.

That all being said, I decided it was time I healed myself on these matters of UFOs and the close encounters. There comes a time to let go, but at the same time learn and take a lesson from that event. Our journey as humans is not to just go along and not participate in humanity. Our involvement in our connections is not just to each other, but also to the planet we inhabit. As I said in an interview, You look out and see the blue skies and know that the top of the blue skies is not where this all ends. It goes on, and on, and on, and on, and on. What we have here, the air we breathe, the planet we live on, we have to take care of because we are not jumping off to a new planet any time soon. We don't have that technology, not yet anyways. We have to take care of what we have right here and right now.

Perhaps in time we will go far beyond this planet, but we need to use the time now to preserve human existence. This global climate change is real and we better get real about our changes to save this planet. I think that if we don't change our ways and protect this planet, then the one thing we have to get to other planets will be lost forever. We need time and the willingness to learn and develop our science for the betterment of humankind. To do so, we have to be around long enough to get to that point. Right now, according to scientist, we are on a destructive course through global pollution. We are all to blame, some more than others, but we share the blame. Each one of us has to chip in, in any way we can. So go plant a tree or find ways to cut down on pollution. Be the change, no matter how small.

To me, it is clear that for humans to survive and carry on, there has to be change, and we have to be that change! We need to look at the world and realize we are more alike than different. This has never been more true than today as the world is facing this horrific pandemic with Covid-19. Does the virus care what nation you are from, what country you reside in, the color of your skin, or your age or sex? Of course not.

How can we get things done, such as turn around this environment or combat a deadly virus, if we are so busy hating one another? If aliens from other worlds came here, do you think they give a damn about the border between the United States and Mexico, or any other country? Get real. The answer is a resounding no! Do you think they would care what race or religion you are? I will go out on a limb and say no to this as well. Life is about existence and the ability to expand our knowledge is dependent on how we treat our planet and our fellow humans. Humanity is about caring how we exist, not just for ourselves but those around us, even strangers. We only do so by letting go of hate, and understanding our symbiotic relationships in both a macro and micro way. This is how I wish to lead my life: with an open mind and heart not just for humans, but to others who travel the galaxies as well.

My belief is that humans have souls, and have the capability to care and are touched by the act of caring, but only if we reach out and try. So if you really want to know what I think about aliens and the 1969 event, OK. They left a message implanted in my brain to pass along. This very message: to wake up and start caring about earth and fellow humans as if our lives depended upon these our actions, because they do.

I was given a vision of another planet with the examples of how to exist as a species. Are they human-like on that planet? Well, that depends on our definition. Their capabilities far exceeded those of average humans, not just in mental telepathy, but the ability to love unconditionally. On that September 1, 1969, night, those aliens could have killed me if they wanted, but that was not their purpose, and so I lived. They could have the second time but they did not, and so I lived and looked for answers. All these contacts, for what purpose? The answer was for me and others to pass along that message and I do hope you are listening very carefully.

Here we are in 2020, and astronomers in the field of radio astronomy have traced what they call fast radio bursts (FRB). Although this is a more recent discovery, the fact the signals are being sent out a mere half-billion light years from earth brings more questions than answers. That is what is needed, both curiosity and an open mind. There was a time this would have been considered a pipe dream, but here in the year 2020, data seems to be discovered at a faster and faster pace. As they say, you have be in it to win it. For humans to survive and move on, perhaps to other worlds, we have to survive the stupidity of selfish destruction and wars and pollution.

That night and the event two weeks later left me with the knowledge that there was more to this world than the selfish wars we fight or our careless behavior as stewards of this planet. Think about how we have spent nearly thirty-two million dollars per day on war since 2001, allowing us to shower hate upon our fellow humans. What a waste of all human resources. Then there is the way we treat our planet, polluting the earth, ourselves, and the waters we drink. Oh, for the love of God, think about that one too.

We pollute the water we drink. Come on people, we are about 70% water. Air and water are not overrated, they are existence and in effect we are killing ourselves, the animals, plants, and life itself. So when some politician tries to sell some bullshit that the environment is not our top concern, you know that person is blind to the truth. This is not about being conservative or liberal, this is about being a human being. Care as if your children's children's lives depended upon this fact of protecting the earth.

I was blessed to have had visions, to have been shown that there is life past this planet that we live on. I endured years of criticism and painful mockery when I told about that fateful night of my first encounter. Oh, yes, the things people would say to me. Perhaps it was because of their fear that we are not alone and we are being watched. Why do you think that for all these years, governments have tried to dismiss the existence of UFOs and aliens? Perhaps so people do not freak out. Oh, my gosh, freak out they would.

Take, for example, on October 30, 1938, a twenty-three-year old Orson Welles put on his broadcast of *The War of The Worlds* radio show. This was at time of the golden age of radio and when people heard the broadcast, they were really scared. Years after my close encounter, I was talking about the subject of UFOs with my favorite Aunt Gladys. I remember my Aunt Gladys telling me she came in right after the broadcast had started and thought martians were going to be in the Berkshires.

She said, Oh, Tommy, this scared the bejesus out of me. I said, Pa, get your guns ready. Of course, Grandpa waited just a while longer before calming her down and telling her that this was not a news broadcast, but rather a show. She continued, Tommy, at that moment I was mad as a hornet at that show, and pretty mad at Pa, too, for letting it go that long before telling me!

I imagine she was not alone that night in her fear of impending doom. However, there was a point there; while we fight each other, war after war, we don't consider what or who else is out there. President Ronald Reagan, on September 21, 1987, addressed the United Nations with his speech on aliens and peace. He stated, "In our obsession with antagonisms of the moment, we often forget how much unites all the members of humanity. Perhaps we need some outside, universal threat to make us recognize this common bond. I occasionally think how quickly our differences worldwide would vanish if we were facing an alien threat from outside this world. And yet, I ask you, is not an alien force already among us? What could be more alien to the universal aspirations of our peoples than war and the threat of war?"

Yes, I was tagged for a reason, just like others were tagged. There are no accidents, only appointments. We are meant to meet and connect so this common bond can pass on the message. We are humans and we need to take care of this planet and each other.

If we cannot get along as humans because of a difference in culture, the faith of our religion, or the color of our skin, then how can we survive for all time? The waste both in resources and human lives is just staggering. We are not an advanced society of humans, even though we think we are. Yes, we are advancing, but at the same time our barbaric nature still holds us back.

My faith that the universe is made up of wonderful abilities was tested over and over; and the most important one is the ability to communicate and express those thoughts telepathically. There is good out there, but for every good force is an equal, opposite force. I believe in that good. What side of humanity are we going to claim as our destiny? That is the question we must ask ourselves. I though about this very question in order to reflect, to think, and even to pray and hope.

I think of sitting by the lakeshore, listing to the waves, admiring each one as it laps upon the shore in perfect rhythm. The beautiful sunset, like a painting of nature, explodes with brightness of oranges and reds, and I hear the crying loon call out one last time before the sun falls to the mountains, giving way to purple, then blue. The moon will replace this perfect painting and sends chills down my spine to the shimmering beauty of your reflection. I breath in the cool summer night air and feel your reflection diving into that water. Oh, that water that gives us life and soothes our souls and drives human spirit. That spirit to love and be loved. Then my eyes are drawn to the heavens above, and one by one the lights appear. Yes, twinkle, twinkle all you little stars. This all made me think, What a perfect place to exist. We are blessed for the existence of earth and our very being, but are we thankful enough? From time to time, a star shoots across the galaxy, like the UFO did that night of September 1, 1969. Knowing they did was more important than the how. Be patient. The how will come in time, oh, all in good time, all in good time. Now I close my eyes and make a wish for our planet earth. I call to you, so hear me; for I hear you now and always have and always will, forevermore, beyond the stars.

Acknowledgements

Special thanks to my caring neighbors, Robby and Carol Baier, for their support on this project. You define what a neighbor should be. To Steve and Helice Picheny, for letting us film on their property for *Unsolved Mysteries* to make the show so special. To the *Unsolved Mysteries* family for reaching out to tell the truth about that historic September 1, 1969, night. What a wonderful job you did. To all my friends who at one point were there on my life journey. Thank you!

About the Author

Tom was born in Great Barrington, Massachusetts, and raised at his family's historic 1835 Warner Homestead. Tom and his wife, Christine, raised their two children in Great Barrington. Not only is Tom the author of his debut work and autobiography, *Beyond The Stars*, Tom is also a historian, poet, and artist. A self-taught watercolor artist, Tom was named on the American Gallery Greatest American Painters list. He also received the James Weldon Johnson Literary Foundation Legacy Award for stellar contributions to Literature and the Arts for his art and poetry. His works are on display in the James Weldon Johnson Institute at Emory University, Fisk University, and the Roswell UFO Museum, as well as in private collections. He was inducted into the Great Barrington Historical Society & Museum. Recently, Tom was featured in the Netflix series, *Unsolved Mysteries,* "Berkshire UFO."

Visit Tom Warner online at tomwarnerbeyondthestars.com.

About the Book

Copyediting and typesetting for *Beyond The Stars* was done by Courtney Larkin Editing. Courtney is an avid reader. She lives on a little family farm in American Fork, Utah, with her husband, Zach, and cat, Winnie. In her free time, she works in her vegetable garden, tends to her houseplants, and dreams up home renovation projects. As a freelance editor, Courtney's favorite part about editing is getting to share in the magic of the story told by the author.

Visit Courtney Larkin Editing at www.larkinediting.com.